Forensics
Current Perspectives from InfoTrac

SECOND EDITION

Prepared by

David Kotajarvi

WADSWORTH
CENGAGE Learning·

Australia • Brazil • Japan • Korea • Mexico • Singapore • Spain •
United Kingdom • United States

For product information and technology assistance, contact us at **Cengage Learning Customer & Sales Support, 1-800-354-9706**

For permission to use material from this text or product, submit all requests online at **www.cengage.com/permissions** Further permissions questions can be emailed to **permissionrequest@cengage.com**

ISBN-13: 978-1-133-31295-6
ISBN-10: 1-133-31295-0

Wadsworth
20 Davis Drive
Belmont, CA 94002-3098
USA

Cengage Learning is a leading provider of customized learning solutions with office locations around the globe, including Singapore, the United Kingdom, Australia, Mexico, Brazil, and Japan. Locate your local office at: **www.cengage.com/global**

Cengage Learning products are represented in Canada by Nelson Education, Ltd.

To learn more about Wadsworth, visit **www.cengage.com/wadsworth**

Purchase any of our products at your local college store or at our preferred online store **www.cengagebrain.com**

Printed in the United States of America
1 2 3 4 5 6 7 16 15 14 13 12

Table of Contents

Part 3: Fingerprint and Trace Evidence   97

Part 4: Detecting Lies

Part 5: The Crime Lab and Ballistics

Preface

The forensics field continues to evolve at a rapid pace. Just think, in 1863 Paul-Jean Coulier showed fingerprints can be used to identify individuals and now millions of prints are on file. In 1870 Alphonse Bertillon created the state of the art way of indentifying criminals by measurements of certain body parts. Especially noteworthy is that in 1895 Polish scientist, Dr. Eduard Piotrowski recognized the importance of blood spatter analysis at crime scenes. DNA was actually first isolated in 1869, but it took until 1985 for Alec Jeffreys to introduce its' enormous value in criminal identification. The United States moved forward in 1932 with the creation of the FBI Crime Lab. Look how far we have come.

Now, every evening you can witness cases being solved in an hour on most network crime scene investigation shows. We have come to the point where nothing surprises us in the forensic arena. The benefits are vast. Innocent people, even some on death row, are being exonerated based on forensic analysis. The data bases of fingerprints and DNA profiles are leading investigators to criminals like never before. In the future there will be other data bases. Perhaps voices, brain waves, and eyes will help in identifying suspects. The sky is the limit.

Another area not mentioned is that of lie detection. Much has been done to find the clues that disclose deception. When Miranda v. Arizona was decided, law enforcement automatically believed that suspects wouldn't talk. Well, suspects continue to respond to the verbal probes of the interrogator and now ways of detecting deceit are becoming more finely tuned.

Part 1: Evidence and the Crime Scene
This portion of the reader is devoted to the new innovations in "scene of crime" evidence processing. New types of evidence are proving to be most important in forensic cases. The "old reliables" like hairs and fibers are discussed as well as lip prints and pollen granules.

Part 2: Blood Evidence
In this section blood evidence is discussed at length. Many issues surrounding DNA have arisen recently which causes the courts to

explore that type of evidence more closely than ever before. In addition, new and streamlined methods of analysis are discussed.

Part 3: Fingerprint and Trace Evidence

Although the spotlight is on DNA at the present time, fingerprints are not completely in the shadows. New and improved ways of lifting prints are always being developed.

Part 4: Detecting Lies

It continues to get harder and harder for suspects to get away with lying to investigators. Many new methods of detecting deceit are discussed in this section. As long as suspects continue to answer questions, investigators will be able to analyze their responses with greater accuracy.

Part 5: The Crime Lab and Ballistics

The crime lab is an essential part of the overall approach to criminal investigation. Crime scene investigators have the benefit of trained professionals utilizing state of the art technology to either eliminate suspects or pinpoint that one person to bring to justice. This arena of forensic investigation is moving forward at a frantic pace.

It is hoped this reader will assist the student in understanding the ever-changing forensic aspects of criminal investigation and bring them up to date on the latest and greatest, as well as inspire the use of their imagination.

David Kotajarvi
Lakeshore Technical College, Retired

Part 1

EVIDENCE AND THE CRIME SCENE

1

Forensic Scientist Describes Crime-Scene Processing at Waseca Murder Site

Janice Gregorson

It was 4 a.m. when Gary Walton got a call from authorities in Waseca County. There was a double homicide. They needed the crime scene team. Walton, a forensic scientist with the Minnesota Bureau of Criminal Apprehension, heads one of the BCA's crime scene response teams that go throughout the state to process crime scenes for local law enforcement agencies. In 2007, crime scene teams processed 74 such scenes related to homicides and officer-involved shootings.

One of those was in rural Waseca County, where Tracy Kruger, 40, and his son, Alec, 13, were shot to death in their rural Waseca home. Hilary Kruger was critically injured. Walton, who lives in the Twin Cities, assembled his team of specialists, and they headed to the area, bringing one of the agency's mobile crime scene lab units.

Walton testified Thursday at the trial of Michael Stanley Zabawa, 26, who is charged with murder and attempted murder; Zabawa denies the

---

Source: Forensic scientist describes crime-scene processing at Waseca murder site. Post-Bulletin, March 6, 2009.

allegations. The trial was moved to Olmsted County due to pretrial publicity in Waseca County. Walton was on the witness stand the entire day, telling jurors in detail how scenes are processed and how evidence is gathered and documented. In the end, he said, no evidence was found inside the Kruger home linking Zabawa to the crime. Walton has been with the BCA since 1983, working in the latent print section. He also is one of the team leaders responding to process crime scenes.

In the early morning hours of Feb. 3, he said, the temperatures were below zero and there were wind gusts up to 50 mph. Team members learned that there were essentially three areas that needed processing -- the Kruger residence, a pickup truck belonging to Zabawa stuck in a snowbank near the Kruger home and the Kruger's own SUV, which was stuck in the ditch across from the pickup truck; a pickup stolen from another neighbor's home that turned up in Matawan, where Zabawa lived; and the Zabawa residence. Before they could enter the Kruger home, they had to make sure law enforcement had obtained a search warrant. The same was true of the vehicles and the Zabawa residence. Walton split up his team, telling jurors that he sent some to Matawan, and he and others stayed at the Kruger residence. There were shoeprints in the snow outside the Kruger residence, by the vehicles, near the neighbor's home and in Matawan that needed to be documented before they were destroyed by the blustery weather to see if the treads matched; distances had to be measured. Walton told jurors he was the first from his crew to enter the Kruger home and did a walk-through, dropping numbered evidence markers at obvious items he didn't want destroyed before they were documented. Those included possible blood stains, shell fragments, spent shell casings, and unfired slugs. Then the team's photographer was sent in to take a video of the entire scene, followed by what could have been hundreds of still pictures. "We record everything in the crime scene before anything is moved," he explained to jurors. Jurors saw those pictures and the video of the crime scene, taken before anything, even the bodies, were removed.

They saw pictures of the house, the various rooms, staircases leading to the upper-level bedrooms, the bedrooms, areas damaged by gunfire, the basement area where authorities say the murder weapon was taken from a gun cabinet, and boxes of various types of ammunition that were strewn on the floor. Photographs and videos also were taken outside, showing the roads were the vehicles were found in the ditches, the driveway approach to the Kruger home, the path of footprints, the property of the neighbor whose truck was stolen, and more footprints.

The vehicles weren't searched until Monday, Feb. 5, he said, after they were moved to a secure location by law enforcement. Once collected, many items typically are subject to further analysis, such as DNA testing, at the crime lab in St. Paul, he said. Dusting for latent prints is done; smaller items, such as shell casings and unfired slugs, are put through a process to see if there are prints. The items are put into a super-glue chamber. The glue is heated up 200 degrees and it turns into a gas. The fumes attach themselves to anything in the chamber. No prints were found, he said. None were found on the shotgun, either. Walton told jurors that prints on non-porous surfaces are fragile and easily wiped away. He said that if a person were wearing gloves, there would be no prints. Walton said it took the team until about 3 a.m. the following day to process the scenes. Then, they returned on Monday and processed the vehicles. He testified that the work continued back at the main lab in St. Paul. Jurors will hear more from Walton in coming days.

2

UPDATE: SBI Agent Testifies About Processing Crime Scene at Flowers Home

Francine Sawyer

State witnesses are expected to continue with testimony in the Vaughn Jones double-murder trial Thursday morning.

On Wednesday afternoon, the jury heard testimony from a State Bureau of Investigation agent who processed the crime scene at the home of Richard and Rosa Flowers of Merritt on Jan. 14, 2003.

He told the jurors what evidence he collected at the home and how it was stored.

The agent, Steven Combs, was a crime-scene specialist in January 2003. He is now SBI special agent in charge of the Coastal District in Jacksonville.

Pamlico County Sheriff Billy Sawyer called for SBI assistance to process the crime scene after the bodies were discovered by the Flowerses' grown children, Rodney and Teresa Flowers.

Source: Update: SBI Agent testifies about processing crime scene at Glowers home. Sun Journal, September 27, 2007.

Combs said none of the three bedrooms in the house had been ransacked.

The only bedroom that showed disarray was the one where the body of Richard Flowers was found. He was in his bed, dead with stab wounds. His empty wallet was found in the bedroom.

Rosa Flowers was found near the living room. Her pocketbook had been emptied and items were scattered on the floor.

Combs said he found a blood smear on the front screen door, but lifted no fingerprints and saw no fingerprint patterns to lift for examination.

Most of the afternoon's time was used as dozens of photographs of the crime scene were passed to each juror to examine.

A large portion of court time was used as Combs told jurors how he marks and labels all evidence in order for the chain of evidence not to be disturbed.

Court begins Thursday at 9:30 a.m.

PREVIOUS UPDATE

A pathologist testified this morning that Richard and Rosa Flowers suffered "rage injury" stabbing wounds that were made with more force than needed to kill them.

The pathologist, Dr. Charles Garrett, who works with the state medical examiner's office in Jacksonville, was the first witness in the trial of Vaughn Antonio Jones. Jones is charged with killing the Flowers couple in their home in Merritt in January 2003.

The couple's son and daughter, Rodney and Teresa Flowers, attended court for the first time in the trial. Teresa Flowers wiped tears as the pathologist described the wounds inflicted on her parents.

Garrett performed autopsies on Rosa and Richard Flowers on Jan. 15, 2003.

He said they both died of blood loss from severe stab wounds. He testified that Richard Flowers had an enlarged heart and that one knife wound cut his heart in two.

He described some stab wounds as large--one of 7 inches and one of 4 inches in Richard Flower's chest.

Garrett said there was little blood at the scene because the nature of the internal injuries and gravity acted to keep the blood in the body.

He said Mrs. Flowers appeared to have been hit on the left side of her head, then to have fallen to the floor and been stabbed by someone standing over her.

Garrett could not estimate the time of death. He could offer only a range from 8 to 24 hours prior to his examination of the bodies. He estimated the length of the blade to be a minimum of three to four inches.

He said the large wounds were the result of the knife being plunged into the bodies and pulled.

Mr. Flowers' body was found in his bed and he appeared to have been murdered in his sleep, Garrett said.

Mrs. Flowers was found in the foyer of the house. The pathologist said she had two defense wounds on the back of a forearm, indicating that she had put her arms up to protect herself.

SBI Agent Steven Combs, a crime-scene specialist, also testified. He said that he found a blood smear on the front screen door, but there was no pattern or fingerprints on the door.

He said Mrs. Flowers had apparently been in bed reading a cookbook before she answered the door. He said nothing had been taken from the bedrooms, including jewelry from a jewel box and a $10 bill.

The court broke for lunch about 12:35 p.m. Combs was to continue testifying this afternoon.

The testimony began after prosecution and defense lawyers made opening statements to the jury.

Special prosecutor W. David McFadyen Jr. made the first statement, saying that Garrett would testify that the Flowerses were not just murdered, but that someone had inflicted more wounds than necessary. He said evidence would show that when Jones was questioned after the killings, he never denied that he was in the house or committed the murders.

McFadyen said Pamlico County Sheriff Billy Sawyer was expected to testify about asking Jones why he went to the Flowerses' house the night of the killings. The sheriff is expected to say that Jones answered that he couldn't say, but he never denied going.

McFadyen said: "This trial is not about the Flowerses, but about Vaughn Jones, who sits in this courtroom dressed nicely but showing no indication of the type of people he hung out with."

He told the jurors that they would hear that Jones tested positive for cocaine in the summer of 2002. He said the first story Jones told lawmen was that he was at his mother's house the night of the murders and never left. Jones later told deputies that he left once, and he hesitated but told lawmen that he had left to do drugs, McFadyen said.

However, he said, the state has video of Jones going to a local convenience store two separate times the night of the murders.

McFadyen said testimony is expected from Billy Jewelll, a Pamlico County sheriff's investigator, that he told Jones "if blood is on your jacket, you'll be connected to the murderss" and that Jones replied, "I didn't take my coat inside. I left it in the car."

Jones' court-appointed defense lawyer, Dick McNeil, said that the question in the case is who did it. "The evidence is what's on trial. You will find," he told the jurors, "that the police investigation was poor. There was lack of documentation and confusion. They discussed talking with others but they cannot recall who or when they spoke."

He said no fingerprints of Jones were found at the scene "You will find that they never found blood in his clothing or the car he drove that night."

McNeil said there was no animosity between Jones and the Flowerses. He said Jones was a witness to the Flowerses' will in 2002. "See if the pieces fit," he said. "There's no signed statement, no video, no audio in this day and age. We believe when the evidence is given to you, your job will start in the deliberation. Just because Mr. Jones is a liar does not make him a murderer."

PREVIOUS STORY

Opening statements are set for 9:30 a.m. today in the Vaughn Jones double-murder trial.

A panel of 12 jurors and two alternates was seated Tuesday. The jury selection ended a day of turmoil in which Jones sought for the second time to have his court-appointed lawyer removed.

Court officials had expected the jury selection to take longer. An additional pool of 200 potential jurors had been summoned to appear in Superior Court today.

Jones is charged with murder in the stabbing deaths of Richard and Rosa Flowers of Merritt in Pamlico County. It is the second trial in the case. The first trial ended with a hung jury a year ago.

Jones came to court Tuesday morning and listened as both the defense and prosecution continued jury selection.

In midmorning, Jones sent a note to resident senior Superior Court Judge Ben Alford.

The jury was sent out of the courtroom as Alford read the note.

Jones said in his note that he wanted his court-appointed lawyer, Dick McNeil, off the case. McNeil also asked, for the second day in a row, to be taken off the case because of the animosity between the two of them.

Jones told the court that he did not think he was being represented properly by McNeil. "I have given him information crucial to my case to clear me," Jones told Alford.

"I have information that will clear my name, but he doesn't listen. His decision is not to put up evidence; nothing has been done. I have asked him to file motions. I refuse to let him represent me," Jones said.

Jones told the judge that he wanted to share the information he had but not in front of the state prosecutors, "because they could use it against me."

Alford cleared the courtroom and for about an hour and 20 minutes Jones explained his position and McNeil gave his.

Both men could be overheard talking loudly outside the courtroom but their words could not be understood.

Jones later talked about the hearing in a session he requested with a Sun Journal reporter. McNeil and Jerry Waller, a private investigator working for the defense, attended the session with the reporter.

He first declared his innocence.

"I want to clear my name," Jones said. "The only thing people know is what's been in the newspaper and what people say. I am sorry about the Flowerses and what happened to them. I have been hurting."

The couple were stabbed and beaten in their home in January 2003. Jones was arrested and charged with the murder by Pamlico County sheriff deputies about 12 hours later.

"I want people to listen to the evidence, all of the evidence and they will not get the full evidence in this trial," Jones said.

Spread at the desk he spoke from were manila envelopes full of search warrants and other court papers from the first trial, a year ago in Pamlico County.

"Sixty to 70 DNA samples were taken from blood and fingerprints at the crime scene," Jones said. "My DNA was found on one item. The SBI agent who tested the DNA admitted that there was a mixture of my DNA and Mr. Richard's (Flowers) present."

Jones said he studied search warrants and found that the agent had labeled a blood sample April 4. He said she could not have received the blood sample then. "It was a Sunday and the lab is usually not open on a Sunday," he said.

The agent has since resigned after a long career with the SBI.

Jones said she had not been subpoenaed for the current trial, but was at the first trial and she admitted then that she was wrong.

"I am innocent," he said. "I am concerned about me. I was questioned for three hours after the murder. I wasn't at their home. I was somewhere that I shouldn't have been," Jones said.

He said that he was involved in drug activity at the time of the murder.

"I still don't know why they arrested me; I am innocent," Jones said.

He said during the interview that he had resolved matters with his attorney. "He is very, very good. We could have settled it man to man," Jones said in an even voice.

Jones worked for the Flowers family for several years. He was hired to work at the family's boat-manufacturing company in Merritt after he was released from prison.

Jones had served time after he was convicted of kidnapping and attempted murder of his girlfriend.

Teresa Flowers, daughter of the slain couple, said in an interview in 2003, shortly after the slayings, that her father did not know why Jones had been in prison.

She said in that interview that Jones was a good worker in the boat company. She said her parents gave him extra work around their home.

"He was a fine person," she said.

Flowers said Jones began borrowing money from her parents.

Jones is accused of going to the family home, which is across from the boat yard, around 10 p.m. Jan. 13, 2003, to ask for money.

The prosecution contended in the first trial that Rosa Flowers refused to give Jones money and he became enraged. Jones is accused of grabbing a kitchen knife and killing her in the foyer of the home, then going into the bedroom and killing Richard Flowers.

When their parents did not appear at work at their usual time the next morning Teresa Flowers and her brother, Rodney Flowers, went to the house to see what was keeping them. Their parents were lying in pools of blood.

Jones did not go to work that morning, but in the interview with the Sun Journal on Tuesday he said he did not go to work the day before the murders.

Jones has been in jail since his arrest.

In the first trial, the state sought the death penalty, but this time it is not. The state will ask for two life sentences if Jones is convicted.

During the first trial Jones did not take the stand. The defense offered no witnesses.

The defense team argued in closing statements that the investigators did not thoroughly investigate and did not take proper notes. The defense lawyers also argued that since Jones worked around the Flowers home, his DNA could very well be present.

During the jury selection process this week, McNeil was careful to ask potential jurors if they took proficient notes. He also asked them if they thought good notes were important in their jobs.

Two family members of Jones have been in the courtroom during the jury selection.

W. David McFadyen Jr., special prosecutor for the case, was district attorney for the Craven, Carteret and Pamlico judicial district when the murders were committed.

He later retired but was hired as special prosecutor for this case last year and he is prosecuting the current case.

The Flowerses' son and daughter, Rodney and Teresa Flowers, are expected in court today. They were not in court Monday and Tuesday.

McFadyen told jurors Monday that he had asked them to stay away during the jury selection because of the tight quarters of the courtroom.

The trial is being held in the basement of the Craven County Courthouse annex.

It is expected to last seven to 10 days.

3

Fibers and Dog Hair Evidence: Is It Real Evidence?

An Update on the Atlanta Child Murders

Georgia Jack Mallard

The killing of Atlanta's children captured the attention of the nation and the world. A total of 30 murders were investigated over two years (1979-1981) as being similar and connected and occurring about three to four weeks apart. After this mysterious killing spree of Atlanta's children, teenagers and young adults, the murders stopped after Wayne Williams was identified at 3:00 a.m. on May 22, 1981. At that time, Williams was stopped at the James Jackson Parkway Bridge over the Chattahoochee River when police heard a splash in the river.

The police task force, which was headed by Atlanta police and included FBI and other federal and local police agencies, was unable to catch the

Source: Fibers and dog hair evidence: is it real evidence? (c) 2007 by Jack Mallard. Reprinted by permission of the author. Jack Mallard is a retired Georgia Prosecutor (1967-2007) and may be reached at jackmallard@comcast.net. Since retirement, he has written and published "The Atlanta Child Murders: The Night Stalker," Copyright 2009 Jack Mallard.

16

killer so a decision was made to post guards on rivers where the killer had begun dumping bodies from bridges. The killer had begun removing clothing from the bodies and dumping them in rivers after it had been made known that the crime laboratory was finding unusual trace evidence consisting of fibers and dog hair on the bodies. (1) Six bodies were recovered from the Chattahoochee River and two from the South River within the six months leading up to Williams's arrest. Five of the bodies were pulled from the Chattahoochee river within the last two months of the investigation. Thus, the decision to have guards at the river the night of May 22, 1981, was a costly but good decision.

On that night, a rookie cop under the bridge heard a splash and saw ripples in the water, then looked up and saw the lights of a vehicle begin to move slowly across the bridge. He radioed to his fellow officers above, who saw the vehicle cross, turn around and re-cross the bridge. The vehicle belonging to Wayne Williams was stopped but because no body was seen, was allowed to proceed. Two days later, the body of the last victim of this murder spree, Nathaniel Cater, was recovered a mile downstream. A previous victim, Jimmy Ray Payne, was discovered about three weeks earlier at the same location in the river. These two victims were the subject of the later prosecution of Wayne Williams resulting in two life sentences after a nine-week trial in early 1982. Conviction was followed by 25 years of appeals and public cries of conspiracies and railroading being lobbed against the prosecutors by Williams, his attorneys and supporters, including some of the victims' mothers,: and two long-time police detectives (no longer in law enforcement--one in prison for life for hiring the murderer of his opponent for sheriff).

After Williams was identified at the river, warrants were executed and samples of fibers from his surroundings (home and automobiles) as well as hair from his German shepherd dog were obtained. The crime laboratory immediately began to match the trace evidence from the victims to Williams. After testimony by three of the foremost experts on fiber and hair in North America (Harold A. Deadman of the FBI laboratory, Larry Peterson of the Georgia Bureau of Investigation laboratory, and Dr. Barry Gaudette of the Royal Canadian Mounted Police, Ottawa, Canada) the jury was out only 12 hours before convicting Williams of the two charged murders. The jury also heard evidence from ten of the other uncharged murders as similar transactions evidence (proof by a preponderance of evidence). The extent of the use of fiber and hair evidence, as well as the use of a large number of similarly uncharged murders had never been seen before or since. The lengthy trial, covered by media around the world, consisted of evidence submitted through testimony of about 250 witnesses and almost a thousand exhibits. It ended suddenly after the first day of jury deliberation with a guilty verdict. The highlights of the circumstantial case were the linkage of the 12 murders by dog hair and fibers and Williams's testimony. Two days of cross-examination put his character into evidence and portrayed Williams with a Jekyl-Hyde personality. Williams's defense presented about 60 witnesses of their own including opposing expert witnesses.

The many matches of fibers from Williams's surroundings were strong evidence that the victims came in contact with Williams's automobiles, (3) his bedroom (4) and other miscellaneous fibers, but most importantly, with a unique trilobal shaped green fiber. This unique fiber was patented by the Wellman Company and distributed in limited supply for carpet made in Georgia and sold in the Atlanta area, including the Williams's home. The other trace evidence on the bodies, the dog hair, was compared to Williams's dog and found to be similar, but identification of hair was limited in 1982.

Since Williams was convicted, (5) he has steadily maintained his innocence throughout direct appeal, state habeas and federal appeals. Although available in Georgia since the first DNA case was decided by the Georgia Supreme Court in 1990, (6) neither Williams nor his many attorneys had ever requested DNA testing of the dog hair or other evidence until recently, when a request for DNA testing was made to Paul Howard, the present district attorney in Atlanta. DA Howard agreed to the request, and specimens including dog hair were sent to an independent laboratory chosen by the Innocence Project. The University of California (Davis) made the analysis. On June 27, 2007, a report was publicly released by the state's prosecutors with findings that Williams's dog could not be excluded as the contributor of the dog hair found on the five victims submitted for testing (only fibers from five of the 12 cases presented at trial were submitted for testing as a sampling). Only mitochondrial testing could be done, but the DNA tests found that mtDNA sequences obtained from each of the hairs recovered from the five bodies and from the Williams's dog's hair were the same.

The defense team, who had requested the testing, claimed that the report was inconclusive while at the same time saying they were disappointed.

In addition to the dog hairs recovered from the five victims and linked to Williams's dog by the California laboratory, eight hair fragments recovered from one of the cases were sent to the FBI laboratory along with a DNA sample from Williams for analysis and possible DNA testing. The test results, made available August 2, 2007, found that Williams could not be excluded and that Williams was included within the 3.43 percent of the African-American population having the same mitochondrial DNA sequence.

Though we knew that the fiber comparisons were valid and strong evidence of Williams's connections to the victims, only now do we know that his dog would have played a stronger role in his conviction had DNA analysis been available in 1982.

So why would Williams not ask for DNA testing at the first opportunity? He was probably hoping that after so many years the specimens were either lost or degraded, and he could have then claimed that DNA testing would have cleared him had the specimens remained intact. It tells me that for almost 20 years, Williams resisted the temptation to seek DNA testing, knowing what it would do.

ENDNOTES

(1) Unbeknownst to the killer, the crime laboratory continued to recover the same fibers and dog hair from the body hair of the victims after they were stripped and tossed into the river.

(2) Some of the victims' mothers were never able to accept the decision that only two cases were prosecuted and that police closed most of the remaining 30 cases as cleared. Some mothers bought into the defense's cries of railroading. The prosecution decision was based on the bridge incident (and other supporting evidence) after the last victim was discovered downriver two days after the splash coupled with the fact that the body of a previous victim had been found in the same location a few weeks before. A hydrologist from the U.S. Corp of Engineers tested the water current in the river from the bridge to where the bodies were found and concluded that the victims (Payne and Cater) had probably entered the river at the point where Williams's vehicle was seen on the bridge and had traversed from the north side of the river (where the splash was seen) to the south side of the river where the bodies were found a mile downstream. The next ten strongest cases,

uncharged, were selected as representative of the similarity of the murders and used at trial.

(3) Williams always claimed, and testified at trial, that he knew none of the victims. Fibers from the several vehicles owned and rented by Wayne Williams and the Williams family during the two-year murder spree, matched fibers on victims who were murdered at the time Williams had access to those vehicles.

(4) A bedspread and a yellow blanket.

(5) Williams v. State of Georgia, 251 Ga. 749, 312 SE2d 40 (1983).

(6) Caldwell v. The State, 260 Ga. 278; 393 SE2d 436. This case was prosecuted in 1990 by NDAA Executive Director Tom Charron during his tenure as the Cobb Judicial Circuit district attorney and by his chief assistant, Jack Mallard.

Jack Mallard is a former Georgia chief assistant district attorney (1967-2007) and is now retired. He may be reached at jackmallard@comcast.net.

4

Luminous Lip-Prints as Criminal Evidence

Ana Castello; Mercedes Alvarez-Segui; Fernando Verdu

ABSTRACT

Luminescence is specially a useful property for the search of invisible evidences at the scene of a crime. In the latent fingerprints particular case, there are at one's disposal fluorescent reagents for their localization. The study of latent lip prints (that is lip prints from protective lipstick, or permanent or long-lasting lipstick that do not leave any visible marks) is more recent than fingerprints study. Because of the different composition of both types of prints, different reagents have been tried out on their developing. Although, lysochromes are particularly useful reagents to obtain latent lip prints, it may occur on coloured or multicoloured surfaces, the developing is not perceived due to contrast problems between the reagent and the surface where the print is searched. Again, luminescence offers the possibility to solve this problem. Nile Red is being studied as a potential developer for latent lip prints. The results on very old prints (over 1 year) indicate that this reagent is highly efficient to get latent lip prints.

Source: Reprinted from Forensic Science International, v155 i2-3 p185, December 20, 1995. Luminous lip-prints as criminal evidence by Ana Castello, Mercedes Alvarez-Segui and Fernando Verdu, (c) 1995 with permission from Elsevier.

1. INTRODUCTION

Luminescence is specially a useful property for the search of invisible evidences at the scene of a crime. The forensic lights make it possible localizing both biological and non-biological fluid stains, which are invisible to the naked eye [1]. There are also at one's disposal fluorescent reagents for the localization of latent fingerprints [2]. Since, the technique requires to get and study minimal DNA samples, the search of latent evidences is more and more important and it must be exhaustive.

In the prints particular case, it must talk about their double identification power. On the one hand, the margin settings techniques allow their study by eliminating the interferences because of the support, so that basic facts for identification can be got. On the other hand, the possibility of getting DNA from a print increases this indication importance [3].

Although they are less investigated, this double ability for identification is also on lip prints [4-6]. The study of latent lip prints (that is lip prints from protective lipstick, or permanent or long-lasting lipstick that do not leave any visible marks) is more recent than fingerprints study. Because of the different composition of both types of prints, different reagents have been tried out on their developing. Although lysochromes are particularly useful reagents to obtain latent lip prints [7], it may occur that, on coloured or multicoloured surfaces, the developing is not perceived due to contrast problems between the reagent and the surface where the lip print is searched. Again, luminescence offers the possibility to solve this problem. Fluorescent reagents that are been used for fingerprints development were tested in the latent lip prints developing. Results show that it could obtain a medium quality developing for latent lip prints up to 60-day-old [8]. The investigation continued with the goal of search for specific reagents for this type of prints (lip prints), and also that they make possible the development of older prints. Nile Red is being studied as a potential developer for latent lip prints. This reagent has been used for the study of lipids in histopathology [9] and also for the quantifying lipids on thin-layer chromatograms [10]. To value its possible usefulness for developing latent lip prints on multicoloured porous surfaces, some previous tests were made, according to the following experimental procedure.

2. MATERIALS AND METHODS

2.1. Materials

--Supports for fingerprints impressions: colour paper napkins, coloured cotton and satin cloths.

--Standard protective lipstick.

--Long-lasting lipstick (Lipfinity, Max Factor[R] no. 19).

--Dark storage bottles, brushes, fuming chamber, glassware, dark chamber, UV protective glasses.

--Ultraviolet light that works between 320 and 400 nm.

--Bluemaxx[TM] (alternate light source that works between 390 and 520 nm).

2.2. Methods

2.2.1. Sample preparation

They used latent lip prints (from protective lipstick and permanent lipstick) that were available at the laboratory, which had not been used in previous trials (odds and ends). That is, prints over 1-year-old that were formed on porous surfaces particularly difficult to develop, specifically colour paper napkins and coloured cotton and satin cloths. These prints were made applying the lipstick (protective or permanent) on volunteers. The manufacturers' recommended time (5 min) for fixation was waited and lip impressions were made on the supports, using sustained pressure for 3 s.

These prints had been left on a table without any kind of protection.

2.2.2. Reagent preparation

So as to prepare, the reagent in solution are taken as a reference concentration levels as seen at the bibliography [9,10]. For this work concentrations were calculated in preliminary tests (results show that Nile Red is effective with low concentrations): Nile Red solution (1 [micro]g/ml) for 100 ml, dissolve 0.1 mg Nile Red in 100 ml ethanol.

2.2.3. Developing

The developing was tried with the reagent in powder and as a solution with ethanol (concentration 1 [micro]g/ml). The developing procedure is very simple. By using a brush or a piece of cotton (for reagent in solution), apply carefully the reagent on the surface where the attempt is being made to locate the latent lip print. For visualizing the print, were used UV-light and an alternate light source (Bluemaxx[TM]).

3. RESULTS

The results are shown on Table 1 (BL, Bluemaxx[TM] light; UV, ultraviolet light; (+), good development; (-), bad development) and they have been very promising. For all the prints has been obtained with a good quality development (a good quality development means that can notice the shape and the outline, as well as the lips lines and wrinkles) and therefore, useful for identification. This result comes out with reagent in powder and also in solution, and the prints can be seen with both types of light. These results on very old prints (over 1 year) indicate that this reagent is highly efficient to get latent lip prints.

4. CONCLUSION

Considering the results obtained, it is already possible to affirm that Nile Red is a very efficient way for searching and developing this kind of traces.

The authors plan to continue this investigation in a more detailed fashion, studying a larger quantity of prints and more variation of surfaces and developing times. Also the possibility of using these reagents on fingerprints and latent lip prints produced without lipsticks ("normal" lipmarks) should be studied.

References Omitted

Table 1

Results after developing old latent prints produced by protective lipstick or permanent lipstick on different porous surfaces

Surface	Lipstick	Developing time (days)
Napkin (blue)	Permanent lipstick	430
Napkin (blue)	Protective lipstick	370
Napkin (red)	Permanent lipstick	580
Napkin (red)	Protective lipstick	580
Cotton cloth (black)	Protective lipstick	370
Satin cloth (black)	Protective lipstick	370
Satin cloth (red)	Permanent lipstick	410
Satin cloth (red)	Protective lipstick	410

Surface	Nile Red (powder)		Nile Red (solution)	
	BL	UV	BL	UV
Napkin (blue)	+	+	+	+
Napkin (blue)	+	+	+	+
Napkin (red)	+	+	+	+
Napkin (red)	+	+	+	+
Cotton cloth (black)	+	+	+	+
Satin cloth (black)	+	+	+	+
Satin cloth (red)	+	+	+	+
Satin cloth (red)	+	+	+	+

5

Digging Up Clues
Research on Buried Blow Flies Will Help Crime Scene Investigators

Matt Shipman

When investigating a murder, every clue helps. New research from North Carolina State University sheds light on how -- and whether -- blow flies survive when buried underground during their development. It's an advance that will help forensic investigators understand how long a body may have been left above ground before being buried -- or possibly whether remains were moved from one grave to another.

"Blow flies are probably the most important insects to forensic entomology," says Dr. Wes Watson, a professor of entomology at NC State and co-author of a paper describing the research. "They are usually the first insects to arrive after an animal -- or a person -- has died."

These flies can arrive at a body in less than 10 minutes, and lay their eggs within an hour. These eggs hatch into larvae -- or maggots -- that

Source: Digging Up Clues: Research On Buried Blow Flies Will Help Crime Scene Investigators by Matt Shipman, November 1, 2011. Reprinted by permission of the author.

25

go through three stages, called instars, before they're ready to turn into adults. Near the end of the third instar, if the body is above ground, the larvae crawl up to 40 yards away from the remains and burrow as much as six inches into the ground to pupate. The pupa is similar to the cocoons used by moths, where the larvae turn into adults. The fully developed fly emerges from the pupa three to five days later and the cycle repeats itself.

Improving our understanding of blow flies can give investigators clues on how a body is handled after a murder.

Understanding the life cycle of blow flies is extremely useful for murder investigations. Forensic entomologists, such as Watson, can determine approximately when insects found the corpse based on the blow flies' stage of development and the size of the maggots. This is different from estimating time of death, because multiple factors can influence the time of insect arrival. For example, a body could be stored in an airtight cooler for several days before being dumped in a field.

But while much is known about the development of blow flies when bodies are exposed above ground, Watson and his team wanted to know how their development would be affected if a body was buried after the blow flies had laid their eggs.

To find out, the researchers buried pupae, second instar larvae and third instar larvae from two different blow fly species. The insects were buried at depths of 5 centimeters (cm), 25 cm and 50 cm, because murder victims are usually buried in shallow graves. The researchers also gave the insects beef and pork as a food source.

"We discovered that these insects do survive," Watson says. "Soil, it appears, is not much of a barrier to flies." In fact, when buried under 50 cm of soil, 35 percent of the third instar larvae survived to adulthood and dug their way out of the ground. For third instar larvae buried under 5 cm of soil, the survival rate was 43 percent.

"This gives investigators additional information. We can now tell that a body was on the surface long enough for blow flies to arrive and lay eggs," Watson says, "or that the body may have been moved -- exposing it to blow flies." In fact, this research stemmed directly from questions that arose during a murder investigation, in which a body had been moved from one burial site to another.

The paper, "Blow flies (Diptera: Calliphoridae) survive burial: Evidence of ascending vertical dispersal," is published online by the journal Forensic Science International . The paper was co-authored by Watson; Geoff Balme, a former NC State post-doctoral researcher; Steve Denning, an entomology research specialist at NC State; and Jonathan Cammack, a Ph.D. student at NC State. The research was supported, in part, by the National Institute of Justice.

NC State's Department of Entomology is part of the university's College of Agriculture and Life Sciences.

-shipman-

Note to Editors: The study abstract follows.

"Blow flies (Diptera: Calliphoridae) survive burial: Evidence of ascending vertical dispersal"

Authors : G.R. Balme, S.S. Denning, J.A. Cammack, D.W. Watson, North Carolina State University

Published : Online, Forensic Science International

Abstract: This study was undertaken to determine if immature blow flies could complete development following burial and emerge from the soil as adults. Two species of blow flies, Cochliomyia macellaria and Protophormia terraenovae, were placed at three depths and at three different life stages, in a simulated burial to evaluate the impact of soil on ascending vertical dispersal and fly survival. In soil columns, immature stages of each species were covered with 5, 25 and 50 cm of soil. Emerging adult flies of both species reached the surface from all depths at all three immature stages (2nd instar, 3rd instar and pupae). At the 50-cm depth, flies were least successful in reaching the surface when buried as pupae and most successful as late 3rd instar larvae (prepupae). Collectively, more adult flies emerged from the soil if buried as 3rd instars (79.6%) than either 2nd instars or pupae (59.6% and 59.3%, respectively ($F_{2,159} = 14.76$, $P < 0.0001$)). Similarly, at shallow burial depths of 5 and 25 cm, 75.6% and 70.4% of the adults successfully reached the surface, compared with 52.6% at the 50-cm depth (F2,159 = 15.95, P < 0.0001). Second instars demonstrated ascending vertical dispersal behaviours in the soil column by pupating closer to the surface. Nearly half (46.6%) of the C. macellaria 2nd instars buried in 25 cm of soil pupated nearer to the surface. Similarly, 45.4% of the P. terraenovae 2nd instars pupated nearer to the surface. When buried at 50 cm, approximately 25% of 2nd instars of both species pupated nearer to the surface. When 3rd instars of C. macellaria and P. terraenovae were buried at 120 cm, 40% and 4.3% of the adults, respectively, successfully reached the soil surface.

Dr. Wes Watson 919.513.2028

6

An Unusual Appearance of a Common Pollen Type Indicates the Scene of the Crime

D.C. Mildenhall

ABSTRACT

Forensic palynology is a useful source of evidence in cases of violence committed in the open. A young girl was grabbed off the street, threatened and brutally raped. During the investigation the exact place of the rape became an issue. Growing around the scene identified by the victim were shrubs identified as Coprosma, a common New Zealand plant and one that produces abundant, easily wind- dispersed pollen. Abundant Coprosma pollen was found at the scene. The pollen were unusual in that the site was very damp, encouraging fungal growth, and fungal hyphae had penetrated the pores of many of the tricolporate pollen grains. Some grains had fungal spores inside. Coprosma pollen identical in preservational characteristics and morphology to those from the scene and containing fungal hyphae and spores were found in considerable numbers on the victim's clothes. This and rare Coprosma pollen grains and fungal remains recovered

---

Source: Reprinted from Forensic Science International, v136 i3 p236(5), November 22, 2006. An unusual appearance of a common pollen type indicates the scene of the crime by D.C. Mildenhall, (c) 2006 with permission from Elsevier.

from vaginal swabs provided evidence that she had been at the scene where she claimed to have been raped.

The diversity of pollen types recovered from the clothing in this case provides further evidence of the usefulness of clothing in picking up and retaining pollen from crime scenes and that obvious staining on clothes is not a pre-requisite for good pollen recovery. It also demonstrates the importance of collecting samples from different parts of the same garment in order to get a full picture of events since different parts of a garment can come into contact with different plants or different parts of the ground in a scuffle. It is also demonstrated that significant evidential material can be collected from the body, in this case from vaginal swabs from the victim. Forensic palynology should be considered in every case of violent assault, especially, but not exclusively, when having occurred in an open area subject to extensive pollen settlement.

1. INTRODUCTION

Research on the distribution of spores and pollen from source relevant to forensic cases has shown that pollen numbers decrease very rapidly from source giving a clue as to how close to a pollen source a crime has been committed [1]. Since many outdoor scenes have numerous pollen and spore sources from large trees to small herbs and bryophytes it is possible in some cases to build up an exact knowledge of where an event has occurred. In the case history described in this paper the exact location of a criminal act was indicated not by the pollen content of the site as a whole, although that was a factor, but by the unusual condition of the dominant pollen type found at the scene. This is rare in such investigations, although the preserved state of recovered spores and pollen is always important, as most crimes, including rapes, are usually committed in drier environments.

Pollen grains by virtue of their very small size, averaging about 25-40 [micro]m, easily adhere to clothing, hair, even to enamel painted wood. Many plants produce large numbers of pollen in their flowering season and many of these are highly resistant to chemical and biological degradation.

Forensic palynology can be a strong source of evidence in cases of rape, murder and other forms of violence, particularly if the assaults occur in the open [2-6], but even if they occur in buildings [7]. Pollen grains are not only recovered from areas of obvious soiling on victim's or suspect's clothing but can become embedded into clothing without leaving any stain visible to the naked eye [2,6].

2. THE CRIME

The information presented here is but a small part of the total evidence presented in the eventual trial and the scenario is based on the information given to the Police by the suspect and verified, as much as it can be verified, by subsequent investigations. Following usual convention, when the term pollen is used it also includes spores from ferns and fern allies.

It was early Sunday morning at the beginning of winter (early June) in a suburb of New Zealand's largest city, Auckland. A teenage girl was walking home after attending a party. She noticed a man walking towards her from the opposite direction. Something must have alerted her because she crossed the road so that she did not pass him on the same side of the street. A little while later she was grabbed from behind and assaulted. Then she was dragged into the bushes lining nearby walls adjoining two factories (Fig. 1) and told that unless she co-operated she would have her throat slit. The assailant gave the victim to understand that he also had a gun. She recognized the man as the person she had avoided earlier. She was forced to perform oral sex on the offender and to take her trousers and underpants off. She was then raped and taken by vehicle to an unknown address where she was raped four times, including anal sex. She was then driven a short distance and dumped on the side of the road near her home before disappearing. While in the car both to and from the unknown address the victim was told to keep her eyes closed "or else".

A Police investigation followed when a complaint was made and a suspect apprehended a few days later. During the investigation it became apparent that the site of the initial attack was going to be an issue in the case. The scene of this initial rape, as identified by the victim, was behind bushes against factory walls (Fig. 1). The bushes consisted of Coprosma and araliads and the ground was covered with abandoned protest signs. The area was damp and secluded.

The forensic palynologist was called into to see if it could be established if the initial sexual assault took place at the scene described by the victim, based on samples already collected by the Police shortly after the assault and taken from the clothes by forensic scientists from the Institute of Environmental Science and Research Limited. This Institute has the role in New Zealand of providing most forensic services to both defense and prosecution. The palynologist did not have an opportunity to visit the crime scene. If this scene could be shown to have been involved then additional serious charges could then be laid against the assailant, and the victim's outline of events would be stronger when presented in court.

The samples collected consisted of swabs from the natal cleft and vulva of the victim, shakings from a jacket she was wearing, cut out patches of light soiling from the jeans she was wearing and a control sample from the scene collected 3 days after the assault. Additional control samples leading away from the prime site would have been collected if the initial sample had not subsequently shown a positive result.

3. PALYNOLOGY

The control sample from the site identified by the victim as being the scene of the initial rape contained abundant pollen, fly ash, microthyriaceous germlings, and fungal spores and hyphae. Microthyriaceous germlings are small, ectoparasitic, peltate fungi, often found on leaves of higher plants, and common in palynological residues, particularly from tropical to warm temperate regions [8,9]. The dominant pollen type was from Coprosma (75%). A further 15% of the assemblage consisted of Cyathea (tree fern spores), Phyllocladus (celery pine, a New Zealand native conifer), Pinus (introduced pine), and Taraxacum (dandelion-type) (Table 1). Some pollen grains at the scene had been under fungal attack and had fungal hyphae growing in them, especially the Coprosma pollen (Fig. 2a). It is possible that these grains were the previous season's pollen rain as many of the grains under fungal attack were less well preserved than most of the grains present.

The relative absence of pollen of the family Araliaceae was not surprising as many New Zealand araliads use insects as a prime pollen transport mechanism rather than wind. Thus, the presence of an araliad at the scene does not mean that the area around would contain many araliad pollen grains and as such this pollen type is always under-represented in pollen assemblages relative to its importance in the surrounding area [10].

The genus Coprosma forms a group of common ornamental garden shrubs found around New Zealand in parks, gardens and also extensively in native and secondary growth bush after logging. There are almost 100 species [11] and a variety of pollen types which tend to grade into each other with the result that it is difficult to determine which species an individual pollen grain of Coprosma originates from. The pollen grains are tricolporate, sometimes tetracolporate, with very short, narrow ectoapertures and a corresponding large polar area. The surface of the pollen grain is often minutely rugulate, often cracked and bearing minute spinules not seen under a light microscope. The exine is more or less 1 [micro]m in thickness with short baculae. The species are so difficult to distinguish that in a recent pollen atlas of New Zealand plants only a general description of the three main subgeneric groups were described [12]. Coprosma produces abundant wind-dispersed pollen and it would be expected that abundant pollen would be found immediately under or very close to flowering or recently flowered plants and as such is often over-represented relative to the importance of the genus in any one area [10]. No flowers existed on the plants near the site and so no direct comparison with site plants was possible in the time frame between the event, depositions, and the High Court trial 10 months later.

The Coprosma grains, both at the scene and on the victim's clothing, were particularly well ornamented, with a clear baculate tectum, short, narrow ectoapertures, and of relatively large size, with very few tetracolporate types present (Fig. 2a and c).

The samples from the victim's jeans and jacket were not expected to provide a pollen assemblage identical to that from the scene. It was not possible to process scrapings of mud off the jeans; the complete pieces cut out of the jeans had to be processed as separate units. Pollen on clothing tends to reflect the previous history of each individual item, thus it was not expected that each sample from the jeans and the one sample from the jacket would produce the same pollen assemblage. The historical pollen would be extracted along with the more recent arrivals. The clothing provided a large and diverse assemblage of pollen types. The jacket contained numerous pollen types not found at the scene of the rape but it did contain abundant Coprosma pollen (25%), fly ash, microthyriaceous germlings and abundant fungal hyphae. The Coprosma pollen was conspicuous in that it had been attacked by fungal hyphae and the pollen were morphologically identical to those found at the scene.

The samples from the jeans worn by the victim were quite different depending on where on the jeans they had been collected. However, all were similar in containing Coprosma pollen grains that were under fungal attack (Fig. 2c), as well as microthyriaceous germlings, fungal hyphae, and fly ash. The sample from the left thigh area of the jeans contained 22% Coprosma pollen, and was similar in content to the sample from the left calf area which had 26% Coprosma pollen (Table 1). The sample from the right knee, as expected given the scenario developed, showed a greater relationship to the control sample, with 86% Coprosma pollen identical in morphology to those found at the scene, but lacked abundant Taraxacum pollen.

Considering the high percentage of Coprosma pollen, the percentages of Phyllocladus and Pinus were similar to the control. Some of the Coprosma pollen grains were still in tetrads indicating that the jeans had been in close connection with a Coprosma plant that was shedding pollen grains under fungal attack, either before shedding or immediately after. This sample was also far less diverse than samples from higher up the jeans (calf and thigh). This was attributed to the fact that the knees were far more worn than the calf or thigh areas and would not have been able to hold such a diverse pollen assemblage.

The relative absence of Taraxacum pollen was not considered significant. Experience has shown that dandelion-type pollen (and many other pollen types, especially those from small herbaceous plants) varies markedly over very short distances and that a presence in more than trace amounts means that the source plant is close to where the sample originated.

Only rare pollen grains and spores from fungi were recovered from the medical swabs from the vulva and natal cleft of the victim. Swabs from the former, however, contained a number of microthyriaceous germlings which could have come from the scene, fly ash, and fungal spores. The other rare pollen could have come from any source. Fly ash was abundant at the scene, but again this material could have come from any source. The swab from the natal cleft contained a small number of pollen grains including two Coprosma grains (Fig. 2a) in a similar preservational condition to those recovered from the scene.

4. DISCUSSION

Coprosma pollen appears in almost all forensic cases in New Zealand, the genus is so widespread in native forest, scrubland, and gardens. Such pollen types with fungal hyphae inside them have not been seen before in previous forensic cases so the occurrence of such grains at the scene and on the clothing was strong evidence for the jeans and jacket having been at the scene of the rape. Also the morphology of the grains was identical between scene and victim's clothing.

The evidence from swabs from the victim's vulva and natal cleft was also strong. The swab from the natal cleft contained Coprosma pollen of identical morphology and preservational condition as those at the scene and as such was consistent with the scene. It was not possible to provide statistical evidence determining the number of females in New Zealand likely to have such pollen grains in their natal cleft, but it is highly unlikely that a woman exercising normal hygienic practices would have such material in their natal cleft. Similarly, it is highly unlikely that a woman would have numerous microthyriaceous germlings, from fungi normally growing on leaves, in her vulva.

What is obvious from this case is the importance of collecting evidential forensic palynological evidence from different sources including both clothing and body of the victim. Different parts of individual garments, especially trousers in this case, need to be sampled. The samples from the left calf and thigh contained abundant pollen (not positively identified in this case as similar pollen were rare or absent from the scene) listed as Rosaceae (Table 1). If any one of these two samples had been the only sample collected from the trousers then comparisons with the scene would have been made much more difficult. Clearly these pollen grains had come from some other source and for some reason were rare on the knees. Experience has shown that trousers contain a different pollen profile the further from the ground samples are taken, often reflecting direct contact with plants of different heights. Similar differences between separate samples from the jacket would have been expected as well.

5. CONCLUSIONS

The diversity of pollen types recovered from clothing in this case provides further evidence of the usefulness of fabrics in picking up and retaining pollen from crime scenes and that obvious staining on clothes is not a pre-requisite for good pollen recovery.

Forensic palynology should be considered in every case of violent assault, especially, but not exclusively, when having occurred in an open area subject to pollen settlement. It is also important to be allowed to take as many samples as possible, including separate samples from individual garments, in order to arrive at a reasonable conclusion. However, it is appreciated that this does involve a monetary cost that often limits the amount of forensic activity that can be undertaken both by defence and prosecution. This often means that a smaller number of control samples are collected than is desirable.

Furthermore, the very few, but significant number of Coprosma pollen grains, fungal spores, and microthyriaceous germlings, from fungi growing in damp soils or on vegetation, obtained from the victim's vulva and natal cleft, show that in similar violent crimes evidence can be obtained from what can appear to be the most unlikely of places.

Pollen evidence is circumstantial in that it may indicate where an event has taken place and who was there, but not that the accused had actually done anything to the victim. However, with the other evidence at hand, including the identification of the offender by the victim and DNA matching, it provided enough direct and circumstantial evidence for the courts to declare that the offender was indeed guilty and that the initial assault had occurred at the place described by the victim. He was sentenced appropriately in the High Court on a charge of kidnapping, threatening to kill, and multiple sexual violations.

Acknowledgments

Samples relevant to this case were supplied to the Institute of Geological and Nuclear Sciences (GNS) by the New Zealand Police via the Institute of Environmental Science and Research, Auckland, New Zealand. The samples were processed by Roger Tremain (GNS). The paper benefited from useful comments by Richard Cook, Erica Crouch, Ian Raine (GNS), Esme Mildenhall (Open Polytechnic of New Zealand), and Pat Wiltshire (University College, London). Fig. 1 was drafted by Philip Carthew (GNS).

References Omitted

Table 1

A summary list of the spores and pollen recovered from the scene and victim's jeans

TAXA	Control	Left Thigh Jeans	Right Knee Jeans	Left Calf Jeans	Jacket Shakings
Cyathea spp.	2	8	1	4	4
Histiopteris incisa	1	2	tr	1	tr
Pteridium esculentum		tr		tr	tr
Smooth monolete spores	x			x	tr
Other trilete spores	x	1	tr	x	tr
Other monolete spores	x			x	
Cupressaceae	2	3	x	2	3
Pinus	5	8	3	4	8
Dacrycarpus dacrydioides	x	tr		tr	
Phyllocladus	4	7	1	11	6
Podocarpus totara	tr	1	tr	2	1
Araliaceae	tr	1		tr	1
Asteraceae	x	1	1	tr	tr
Betula	tr	tr	tr	x	
Buddleia	tr	tr		tr	1
Casuarina	x	1		2	1
Coprosma	75	21	86	26	25
Cyperaceae		tr		1	9
Ligustrum	1	1	tr	1	9
Lonicera	x	tr	tr	tr	1
Malvaceae	tr	tr		x	tr
Metrosideros	x	2	tr	tr	2
Nothofagus fusca-type		tr	tr	x	tr
Plantago spp.	1	8	2	6	7

?Nertera	?	1	tr	tr	tr
Poaceae	1	6	tr	6	5
Rosaceae	tr	18	tr	19	17
salix		tr		tr	tr
Taraxacum-type	4	2	x	5	tr
Other pollen types	1	5		5	4
Total Count	300	350	300	300	300

x = Present but located after count to 300 or 350; ? = uncertain identification; tr = trace (less than 1%). Figures are percentages.

7

Plan Would Let Officers Create a Perimeter around Crime Scenes

Sadie Gurman

Crime scene technicians, police officers and detectives had just finished studying the site of a double shooting in West Homestead early Thursday and were returning to their cars when they heard the sound of gunfire, this time directed at them.

"Two shots were fired in our direction," West Homestead police Chief Christopher Deasy said. "We all turned and ran to the area where they came from," and could smell the gunpowder.

Allegheny County District Attorney Stephen A. Zappala Jr. said the investigators might have been safer had they been joined by officers armed with patrol rifles who could protect the perimeter. He said he is working with Allegheny County police to craft a plan that would make available "a complement of officers" with AR-15 rifles to guard certain suburban crime scenes, such as those that are poorly lit.

Source: Plan would let officers create a perimeter around crime scenes. Pittsburgh Post-Gazette, February 18, 2011.

© 2013 Cengage Learning. All Rights Reserved. May not be scanned, copied or duplicated, or posted to a publicly accessible website, in whole or in part.

Mr. Zappala floated the idea Thursday when he met with several suburban chiefs and a few residents in Homestead. Officers with patrol rifles would be available to help secure crime scenes in smaller municipalities that lack the resources to do so on their own. County police already have the rifles, Mr. Zappala said.

The agency controlling the scene would decide whether the additional firepower is needed.

"It's just a matter of protocol," Mr. Zappala said. The visible presence of the long-range weapons would show those who feel compelled to take aim at detectives that police can "return with deadly force."

County police Superintendent Charles Moffatt said municipalities could request county officers or their rifles or both, and they wouldn't be needed at every scene. Officers who request rifles, though, must be trained to use them.

County detectives on Thursday were still searching for a gunman who shot two Wilkinsburg teens in the 300 block of Walnut Street about 9:30 p.m. Chief Deasy said all three men had arrived there together in a jitney, and when the teens -- ages 16 and 17 -- got out and started walking away, the third man opened fire on them from behind.

One victim ran to Cherry Street, the other to the lot of a BP gas station on Seventh Avenue. The gunman took off in an unknown direction.

Neither victim suffered life-threatening injuries, the chief said. Police don't know if the same person who shot the pair also fired at officers. The gunfire came from about 150 feet away on Sarah Street, as police were packing up to leave. Detectives found no shell casings, Chief Deasy said.

8

Investigating the Future
Lessons from the "Scene of the Crime"

Charles Brass

As practitioners of a relatively young profession, futurists are frequently asked to explain what they do. Often, the askers have some skepticism. I personally have lost track of the number of times people have asked to see my crystal ball or my time machine when I have shown them my business card.

Many people seem to be unable to get their heads around the idea that it is possible to learn something useful about events or situations that have not yet happened. Yet, when archaeologists report on what they have learned, no one doubts their professionalism, despite the fact that they were not at the time and place they are observing.

This is why, when I am asked to explain what a futurist does, I use the analogy of an archaeologist or, for younger audiences, a crime-scene investigator. Most practicing futurists are at least as interested in the past as they are in the future, but my use of this analogy goes far beyond simply acknowledging that how we arrived at the present has a powerful impact on what will happen in the future.

Source: Investigating the future: lessons from the "scene of the crime." The Futurist, Nov-Dec 2011, v45 i6 p47(4). Originally published in The Futurist. Used with permission from the World Future Society (www.wfs.org).

Both crime-scene investigators and futurists are interested in learning more about a time and place remote from themselves, and both use increasingly sophisticated sets of tools and techniques to help them expand their knowledge. Before they begin to use any of these tools, however, they follow a series of protocols that are designed to ensure that they do their job rigorously and that others can validate and replicate their work. This article looks at some of the rules that crime-scene investigators (CSIs) follow. These rules have direct parallels in helping to shape not only good crime-scene analysis, but good futures practice, as well.

DETERMINING THE INVESTIGATION'S BOUNDARIES

The first thing that CSIs do is to define the physical space in which they are interested and then cordon this area off. This is no trivial exercise. The CSIs expect to invest considerable time and energy in examining the interior of that quarantined space, recognizing all the while that drawing too wide a boundary may yield only marginally more knowledge. Similarly, drawing too narrow a boundary will increase the likelihood that important information will be overlooked. In any case, no boundary can possibly capture everything or everybody of interest.

Futurists, too, have to delineate boundaries around the themes in which they and their clients are interested. As good systems thinkers, futurists are acutely aware of the extent to which everything is interconnected, and they are always concerned that important information may lie outside the immediate area of their focus.

They also know (and if they don't, their clients always remind them) that they don't have an infinite amount of time within which to explore the future. Futures work is designed to enhance the quality of decisions made in the present, and clients most often want to make decisions quickly. For instance, those responsible for public-school systems must anticipate numbers of incoming kindergarteners some years in advance, but this is difficult in the absence of detailed information about such things as decisions to open or close local factories, or planned changes in zoning regulations.

The CSI has an advantage over the futurist in that the boundary of an official crime scene is marked with very visible tape that everybody understands and most people respect. Even if futurists are meticulous and explicit about defining the boundaries of a particular assignment, the nature of their work and the people they work with mean these boundaries regularly get challenged or ignored. Nonetheless, most futurists find it very helpful in their consulting work to take time early in the process to discuss, and hopefully agree on, the boundaries within which any particular assignment will take place.

Of course, good CSIs know that a new discovery might at any time cause an expansion of the taped-off area. Similarly, futures work is made easier if the futurist and the client can explicitly acknowledge that some proposed new action is taking the assignment beyond the previously agreed boundaries. In the school system example, chronic flooding in the region may also impact families' relocation decisions, so the futurist's boundaries might need to expand to include environmental factors.

There is more to the tape around a crime scene, however, than just simply defining where the CSI will focus attention. The tape reminds others that the space inside is a special place and needs to be treated carefully.

This is another way in which the CSI has an advantage over the futurist. CSIs can pretty well ensure that no one will enter their area of interest unless they have been invited, and even then they will follow the CSI's rules of conduct. In effect, the CSIs attempt to freeze the crime scene until they complete their investigation.

Futurists' areas of interest can rarely be as conveniently frozen while the analysis takes place. Nonetheless, if people who do continue to move around inside the demarked area are aware that, for the moment, this is a special space, they are more likely to think more carefully about the actions they take. Perhaps the members of the school board might need to be reminded to factor their yet-to-be completed future scanning into their current budget cycle.

For futurists, marking out the territory of interest in a particular investigation includes identifying the people who habitually occupy that territory. Letting all these people know that an investigation is taking place can often reduce the accidental damage done by those who aren't aware of the significance of the space.

Of course, not everyone's motives are pure and wholesome. Both CSIs and futurists need to be aware that some people will deliberately try to mislead or taint the crime scene or the future space.

ANALYZING EVIDENCE OBJECTIVELY

Having drawn a boundary around their area of interest, CSIs then get down to work. They know that their primary role is to carefully notice and document as much as possible. In addition to their five human senses, they bring their experience and a variety of technological tools to help them in this work.

They are acutely aware that their mere presence on the scene changes things, and that their human prejudices and biases color what they notice and how they report on what they notice. They are aware, too, that some of their work is unpleasant, and that it is a natural human reaction to try and cover up some of this unpleasantness.

Futurists, too, are most often outsiders that other people bring in to a situation to help make sense of it. Like any other human beings, too, futurists are prone to bring biases and prejudices to everything they do. Just as the fingerprints of all CSIs and police officers are recorded so they can be eliminated from the investigation, so futurists need to be careful to eliminate as much of their influence on the scene as they can.

Futurists also should know that, whatever specialist expertise they claim to bring, many others on the scene will nonetheless seek to bring their perspectives to the situation. In particular, futurists need to be aware of the natural human tendency to avoid unpleasantness. The best futurists are skilled at presenting the results of their work in such a way that all relevant aspects are given their appropriate weight.

Placing a tape around a crime scene gives the impression that the moment of the crime has been frozen for analysis by the CSI. The skilled investigator, whether CSI or futurist, knows that everything changes, even during an investigation, so the more they know about how things change, the more useful they will be.

In this regard, the training that futurists receive might give them an advantage over the CSIs. Learning to appreciate all the dimensions within which change takes place is an integral part of futurist training, and good futurists are aware that only dead things change in regularly predictable ways.

The CSIs are almost always examining purely physical, geographic space. Futurists, on the other hand, explore landscapes that are shaped and populated by human beings for whom change is an unpredictable inevitability.

CSIs' specialist expertise is most often accepted by all those involved. They can often rely on the legal system both to support their efforts and t,o compel the participation of all those in whom they are interested.

Alas, futurists have no such legal mandate. Where the CSI can usually assume that those who commission their work are genuinely interested in their professional analysis--such as identifying a cause of death or indicating a probable perpetrator--futurists often confront unwilling participants or even clients unwilling to listen to what has been learned.

CSIs are provided with an ever-expanding toolkit, much of which is the result of developments in science and technology. In particular, they have access to many tools that enhance or extend human senses and give precise quantitative data.

Futurists, too, have access to an expanding toolkit. Like the CSIs', much of the futurists' equipment is designed to supplement individual human senses, often by aggregating information across larger populations. Some of the futurist toolkit is also designed to tap into underutilized areas of the human experience, such as myth, metaphor, and worldview. Often, the futurists seek to sharpen human senses by focusing them in a variety of ways. Modern technology enhances the futurist toolkit by allowing the collection, analysis, and interpretation of quantities of data that would otherwise stretch human capability.

Whatever tools are used, both the CSIs and the futurists need to be aware of the limitations of human ability to understand and interpret the information before them. And they also need to be aware that some people have malicious intent and can either inadvertently or consciously taint the data.

STUDYING THE PAST AND STUDYING THE FUTURE

CSIs and futurists are both part of our modern world because human beings are relentlessly interested in the world around them. Since none of us can be everywhere at all times, we are collectively prepared to invest in developing the skills of that special subset of people who can help us make sense of a world we did not, or could not, experience: the past and the future.

Good CSIs know that the past is not a space that anyone can completely understand. No matter how many resources we bring to bear on studying it, our comprehension of the past--even of very recent events-- will always be imperfect. What CSIs expect to do is to work diligently to reduce this imperfection as much as they can.

Futurists can relate to this: The future is also inherently uncertain. They strive to reduce the uncertainties as much as possible by applying systemic and systematic approaches to understanding the future.

There is a final, crucial difference between CSIs and futurists, however. CSIs primarily exist to help others understand what has happened. Futurists are interested in what may happen and are even more interested in what we would like to happen. Futures work is about both understanding the future and creating it.

In The Clock of the Long Now, futurist Stewart Brand wrote: "Our experience of time is asymmetric. We can see the past, but not influence it. We can influence the future, but not see it." He may have been wrong on both counts. Many people behave as though they could influence the past, and we all strive to see the future. What both CSIs and futurists remind us is that doing all these things will be improved if it is done systematically and rigorously. ?

RELATED ARTICLE: Crime-Scene Futurists: Six Rules from CSI

1. Explicitly describe the boundary marking the edges of the space in which you are interested. There often will be physical, temporal, and/or organizational dimensions of this boundary and all need to be identified.

2. Ensure that all the people who normally inhabit this space, or are likely to enter the space during the project, are aware of the project and its aims.

3. Document the current contents of the space in as much detail as time and resources permit.

4. Investigate the provenance of the space with as much diligence as you can.

5. Notice how, and why, the space changes during the project. Look for both the internal and external forces that might explain these changes.

6. Use appropriate tools from your futurist toolkit to begin to tease out the future for the space.

About the Author

Charles Brass is chair of Australia's premier futures organization, the Futures Foundation, which incorporates the professional association for futurists in Australia. E-mail cab@fowf.com.au; Web site www.futuresfoundation.org.au.

Part 2

BLOOD EVIDENCE

9

Forensic Scientist:
DNA Ties Murder Suspect to Troy Killings

Kenneth C. Crowe II

D NA found on a bloody bedsheet ties murder defendant Michael Mosley to the scene where a man and woman were killed in 2002, a prosecution forensic scientist testified Friday. The sample was originally identified as that of a male John Doe following the killings of Sam "Frost" Holley and Arica Lynn Schneider in their Brunswick Road apartment. Russell Gettig, of the New York State Police Forensic Lab, said every two weeks for eight years the John Doe DNA was compared to DNA in the state and national DNA databases. A match with Mosley's DNA was reported on Feb. 23, 2010, and confirmed on March 29, 2010, Gettig said. Mosley, 41, of Averill Park is on trial for first-degree murder and faces up to life in prison if convicted of the torture, beating and stabbing of Holley, 27, and Schneider, 18, on Jan. 26, 2002, in their Brunswick Road apartment. Holley and Mosley sold crack cocaine together, according to testimony Thursday by Shenoll "Ambush" Bruno, who also was part of the drug operation. Defense attorney Terence Kindlon began his cross-examination of Gettig by focusing on a review of various exhibits recovered from the murder scene. These included a lighter, door jams, sweat pants and a broken knife. Officials have said Schneider was not involved in drugs and was in the process of leaving Holley when she died.

Source: Forensic scientist: DNA ties murder suspect to Troy killings, Times Union, May 13, 2011.

51

10

Crime Scene DNA can Lead to Knock on Relative's Door

Jeremy Kohler

What do you tell a detective who says you are genetically related to a criminal and wants to know who you think it might be?

It is not an abstract question. Investigators may soon routinely trace suspects using their relatives' DNA -- a technique that could solve more crimes but that causes critics to fear for innocent people's privacy.

Familial searching is not a new technology, but a new use of an old one. A crime lab worker scouring government databases for a match to an unknown suspect's DNA can sometimes detect a profile with enough similar traits that it might belong to a close relative.

Once police have a family in their cross hairs, they can investigate the members, or even seek samples of relatives' DNA to narrow the suspect pool.

"How can we ignore that?" asks Lt. Kevin Lawson, who supervises the St. Louis County police crime lab.

Source: Crime Scene DNA can lead to knock on relative's door, St. Louis Post-Dispatch, June 17, 2008.

Experts say the technique could put heat on cold cases, increasing the number of hits by 40 percent. Britain, which pioneered the technique, has used it to solve several sensational crimes.

Software used in American crime labs isn't as useful for identifying relatives' DNA as in Britain, experts say. But even if it were, the U.S. is far from reaching consensus on whether the Constitution would allow authorities to probe an innocent person's genes to investigate a crime.

Many believe it could violate the Fourth Amendment's protection from unreasonable search.

The debate has roiled a few Eastern and Western states. Last month, California became the first state to publicly embrace the familial DNA search as a crime-fighting tool. Massachusetts could be next. Maryland is the only state to ban it.

But middle America has heard little about it.

"There has not been a public engagement on whether this practice would be ethically and legally sound, and we think that there should be," said Sara Huston Katsanis, a research analyst for the Genetics and Public Policy Center at Johns Hopkins University in Baltimore.

FAIR TO FAMILIES?

Critics of familial DNA matching, including civil libertarians and defense lawyers, argue against putting whole families under suspicion.

"You need one member of your family to be a bad apple, and now your whole family's life is going to be up for examination," said Cindy Dryden, a St. Louis-based attorney with the Missouri public defender's office who has litigated several trials that hinged on DNA profiling.

St. Louis County Prosecuting Attorney Robert P. McCulloch called familial DNA searching "a great idea" and questioned the logic of its critics.

"Any sort of an investigation does the same thing," he said. "If you have a murder ..."a[degrees], the first person you go to are family members."

He said it's like a red light camera that photographs the back of car, putting a whole family under suspicion for a traffic violation.

"Obviously there are much more serious issues involved, but the rationale is the same," McCulloch said. "The difference is that DNA testing will tell you who was driving the car."

The American Civil Liberties Union has criticized California's decision to go ahead with familial DNA searches.

"I understand the benefit and how it could sometimes result in something good -- finding the supposed killer," said Anthony Rothert, legal director of the ACLU of Eastern Missouri. "But putting innocent people under genetic surveillance, the risk and harm is not necessarily balanced out by an occasional success at finding someone."

For years, Missouri has aggressively collected biological samples from state prisoners -- and Illinois from all convicted felons, regardless of incarceration -- to compare their DNA with evidence in unsolved crimes.

Missouri has collected more than 161,000 profiles of known offenders and 6,500 unknown samples from crime scenes; Illinois has more than 296,000 offender profiles and 15,000 samples from unsolved cases.

But neither state has had any public discussion about whether to search databases for the DNA of suspects' relatives.

As of now, neither state's laws address it, and a canvass of area police departments shows that only the larger ones were aware it was possible.

WAITING FOR COURTS

McCulloch said he and many other prosecutors are watching to see whether the practice survives legal tests in California and Massachusetts.

"This is brand-new, hot off the presses," said Milton Hirsch, a Miami defense attorney who lectures and writes on DNA issues, and who recently briefed an association of Missouri defense attorneys on the technique.

"What always happens, as more states start tinkering, is that a body of law develops from lawyers and judges and law professors, and even the legislatures, if we can wake them up," he said. "But the problem is we are at a juncture where science in this area is moving rapidly ahead of the law."

Until lawmakers give them more direction, workers in the Missouri Highway Patrol's statewide crime lab will, under an interim policy, notify a local police agency if a close partial DNA match is made.

If investigators are interested in the identity of the possible relative, the lab will conduct more tests. If kinship is found to be likely, the investigators will get the name.

So far, just one such notification has been made, according to Susanne Brenneke, who heads the state's Combined DNA Index System. She would not release details but said no one has been convicted.

More such "hits" are likely as the database grows, she said.

"The purpose of having these offender profiles is to help solve crimes, which is why we think we have the mandate to report out these partial matches," Brenneke said.

Although searches could point to suspects' relatives, Brenneke insisted the lab is looking only for a perfect match to an offender, using a stringent search to eliminate almost every other sample.

Missouri does conduct familial DNA searches for relatives of missing persons or unidentified remains, she said.

Lawyers for Illinois State Police are studying the technique and drafting a policy, an agency spokesman said. For now, every partial DNA match would come under close review before being used in an investigation, said Lt. Scott Compton. He would not say whether it's ever happened.

The St. Louis Police Department, whose bustling lab leads the state in matching unsolved cases to known offenders, declined to discuss familial matching. "We're not talking about this with you," said Officer Jeremy Stockmann.

Ed Postawko, chief warrant officer for the St. Louis circuit attorney's office, called it "an interesting topic" and said he was "glad there is some ongoing discussion and interest being raised in this area."

He said he didn't feel comfortable talking about how much his office has studied the technique.

MINORITIES A CONCERN

Some critics say familial DNA techniques could put minorities under greater scrutiny. Blacks make up less than 12 percent of Missouri's population but more than 40 percent of its prisoners. That means a black Missourian would be far more likely than a white one to have a relative's DNA in the offender database.

But some police officials say the need to capture a violent criminal outweighs other considerations.

"If you've got a forcible rape, and the suspect is still at large, it seems important that you'd want to use every tool at your disposal," said Cole County Sheriff Greg White.

In 2006, British police used a familial DNA search to list 43 people who might be related to a serial rapist. The third door they knocked on was the rapist's sister, who had given a DNA sample in a drunken driving case. With police closing in, the suspect confessed to his father.

On the American side of the pond, police have just begun to find criminal suspects through their relatives. In 2005, Kansas police tracking a serial killer obtained a court order to analyze a pap smear from the daughter of their top suspect, Dennis Rader, without her knowledge.

The DNA match was so close that it pointed to her as being the child of the rapist who had called himself BTK -- for bind, torture and kill. The link gave authorities enough evidence to arrest Rader; he immediately confessed he was BTK.

Experts say it's just a matter of time before American labs can better search DNA databases for suspects' relatives.

"And not much time -- weeks, months, perhaps -- before there will be a very good state of the art," said Hirsch, the Miami attorney.

If Missouri were to allow familial DNA searching -- and improve its ability to do it -- more people could be getting a knock on the door from police looking for the whereabouts of a relative.

Said Brenneke, of the Missouri crime lab: "Could it help solve crime? I'm sure it could."

11

Yissum Develops Novel Method for Forensic DNA Profiling

Yissum Research Development Company, the technology transfer company of the Hebrew University of Jerusalem, announced the development and introduction of a novel method for identifying a suspect's DNA even in complex DNA mixtures.

The novel strategy, developed by Prof. Ariel Darvasi from Department of Genetics of the Hebrew University in collaborations with Lev Voskoboinik from the Forensic Biology Laboratory of the Israeli Police, as part of his MSc thesis, consists of checking the DNA mixture and the suspected individual's DNA for 1000-3000 single letter changes (polymorphisms) which are relatively rare in a relevant population.

"DNA profiling has become an indispensable tool in crime investigations, and is used both to convict and acquit suspects," said Yaacov Michlin, CEO of Yissum. "It is therefore of great importance that crime investigators will be able to determine with accuracy whether a suspect is indeed connected to the crime scene. The novel DNA profiling method developed by Prof. Darvasi will enable the police to investigate even complex crime scenes containing DNA from multiple individuals and discern with high reliability the presence or absence of DNA from a specific suspect."

Source: Yissum Introduces a Novel Method for Forensic DNA Profiling. Jerusalem, Israel, November 30, 2010. Copyright 2010. Yissum, Hebrew University Technology Transfer. All rights reserved.

Our DNA consists of long chains comprising various combinations of 4 small molecules, referred to as A, G, C and T. Forensic DNA analysis is based on the fact that the exact DNA "script" of each individual on the planet is unique. The human genome, our DNA, comprises three billion letters, 99.9 percent of which are identical in any two random individuals. Yet the remaining 0.1 percent letters, corresponding to about 30 million possible changes arranged in various combinations, enabling each and every one of us to carry our own individual DNA "barcode". Thus, in a particular position along the DNA chain, one individual will have the letter "A", whereas another will carry the letter "G". These particular DNA letters are termed "polymorphisms".

Current DNA profiling methods check a few such "polymorphic" sites and if they all match exactly to the suspect's DNA, one can establish with extremely high certainty that the DNA found in the crime scene belongs to the suspect. But if the DNA found in the crime scene is a mixture from more than 2 individuals, which is often the case, current DNA analysis methods are inefficient. Prof. Darvasi's invention enables one to establish with a very high level of certainty if a suspect's DNA is present in a mixture of DNA that comprise even up to 10 individuals. The procedure involves analyzing the DNA mixture for 1000-3000 polymorphic sites where DNA letter changes are rare in the population (found only in about 5 percent to 10 percent of the population). Thus, a suspect will carry about 100-200 of these rare letter changes. If the DNA mixture collected in the crime scene does not include the suspect's DNA, there is almost no chance that all of his/her 100-200 specific and rare letters will be present. On the other hand, if all these rare polymorphisms are present, then the only logical explanation is that the mixture included the suspect's DNA. Consequently, the method presented can establish with high certainty whether the suspect's DNA was present or absent in the DNA mixture collected from the scene of the crime.

Yissum Research Development Company of the Hebrew University of Jerusalem was founded to protect and commercialize the Hebrew University's intellectual property.

12

Families and Forensic DNA Profiles

Rebecca Dresser

L aw enforcement officials often turn to DNA identification methods to detect--and rule out--possible offenders. Every state operates its own database of convicted offenders' DNA profiles; some states store profiles of arrested people, too. The Federal Bureau of Investigation maintains a national database of profiles submitted by laboratories across the country.

A few years ago, officials came up with a new way to use DNA profiles in forensic identification. Ordinary searches require an exact match between DNA found at a crime scene and a forensic DNA profile. A partial match means that the profiled individual should not be considered a suspect. But partial matches create another possibility: the crime scene DNA may come from a relative of the individual whose profile is in the database.

The United Kingdom has used partial matches to identify unknown offenders in several high-profile cases, and the technique is gaining traction in the United States. The 2010 identification of a suspected serial killer could accelerate this trend.

Source: Families and forensic DNA profiles by Rebecca Dresser. The Hastings Center Report, May-June 2011 v41 i3 p11 (2).

THE "GRIM SLEEPER"

Last summer, a familial DNA search led police to a man believed to have killed at least ten women in the Los Angeles area. The killings occurred between 1985 and 2007. (Initially, police thought the killer had been inactive for part of that time, and this gave rise to the "Grim Sleeper" epithet.) Prosecutors have charged Lonnie David Franklin, Jr., with the murders.

Before the familial search, efforts to trace DNA found at the crime scenes had been unsuccessful. Franklin's DNA profile was not in the forensic database. Although he had previously been convicted of possessing stolen property, his convictions occurred before California started collecting DNA from people who had committed that offense.

The familial DNA search found a partial match between DNA recovered from the victim's bodies and DNA from an offender whose profile was in the forensic database. The police put together a list of that offender's male relatives, focusing on the ones who lived nearby and were old enough to have committed the murders. This led them to the offender's father, Lonnie David Franklin, Jr. They began tracking Franklin's movements and eventually were able to retrieve his discarded food and utensils from a restaurant. The DNA on those items matched DNA samples from the murder scenes. (1)

California is one of a relatively small group of states with a published policy on partial DNA matches. A 2008 directive from the state attorney general's office authorizes forensic laboratories to report partial matches to police and to conduct DNA searches specifically aimed at identifying an unknown perpetrator's relatives. (2) Maryland has gone in the other direction, enacting a law that prohibits familial DNA searches. Many states lack clear rules on these practices; in others, officials have adopted internal laboratory rules without public disclosure and debate. The FBI's current policy gives states authority over whether to permit partial match searching and reporting. (3)

BENEFITS AND HARMS

Franklin's arrest dramatically illustrates the benefits that familial DNA identification can produce. If his guilt is established, California's familial search will have removed a dangerous killer from the streets and enabled society to punish that killer. Besides helping law enforcement officials apprehend more criminals, familial identification could deter others from future criminal activity. And familial DNA identification could protect innocent people from wrongful arrest and conviction. (4)

On the other side of the equation are the potential harms produced by familial identification. The approach raises several family privacy concerns. The genetic information recorded in forensic databases consists of short DNA stretches with no known role in determining a person's disease susceptibility or behavioral characteristics. But the actual biological samples taken from crime scenes, suspects, and relatives contain much more DNA. Few states explicitly prohibit sample analysis that could reveal information about a person's genetic traits and predispositions. Familial searches can also uncover mistaken beliefs about biological relatedness. Because many states lack clear rules addressing these matters, there is a possibility that law enforcement officials will improperly discover, and disclose, important personal information about families.

Other types of intrusions are likely as well. Police officers pursuing genetic leads will interview relatives of individuals who are partial matches to crime scene DNA, and they will request samples from the relatives. They will engage in surveillance and surreptitious DNA collection, as they did in the Franklin case. Officers will seek information about the relatives from coworkers and neighbors. These actions could have a good result, as they apparently did in the Grim Sleeper case. But innocent people will be targeted in such investigations, too, and they will be targeted purely because they happen to be related to someone whose DNA is in the forensic database.

In the United States, the harms inflicted by familial DNA identification will have a disproportionate impact on African Americans and Latinos. These groups are overrepresented in forensic DNA databases because they are overrepresented in the population of convicted and arrested individuals whose information is included in those databases. Most observers believe that racial and ethnic bias is at least partially responsible for the disproportionate arrest and conviction rates. And as law professor Sonia Suter puts it, "Familial searching threatens to compound these problems and exacerbate racial disparities in the criminal justice system even further." (5) African American and Latino families will bear the brunt of the intrusions associated with familial DNA identification.

These are serious concerns, but they must be considered in the larger context of criminal investigation practices. Police engaged in traditional criminal investigation may interview, observe, and even interrogate a suspect's relatives. Familial DNA identification certainly adds to the potential intrusions, but the technique could also protect relatives of innocent suspects from the intrusions that accompany traditional police investigations. Moreover, the concerns about disproportionate impact must be weighed against the benefits that familial DNA identification could produce for members of socially disadvantaged groups. (6) Members of these groups are often crime victims; indeed, all of Franklin's alleged victims were African American. After he was arrested, victims' families and community advocates expressed great relief and appreciation that a suspect had been identified.

MAXIMIZING BENEFITS, MINIMIZING HARMS

Given its apparent value in solving high-profile criminal cases like Franklin's, law enforcement officials will probably remain enthusiastic about familial DNA identification. Though the approach could face future constitutional challenges, there is a good chance that it will survive such challenges. In previous challenges to forensic DNA identification, courts have ruled against claims that it involves unreasonable searches and seizures prohibited by the Fourth Amendment. Family identification raises distinct constitutional issues, however, and it's possible that courts might object to certain features of the approach. (7)

In the absence of constitutional barriers, legislators and criminal justice officials will determine what policies govern familial DNA identification. The goal should be to maximize the benefits and minimize the harms of this approach. Scholars recommend several policy actions to achieve this goal.

One is for authorities to adopt strict scientific standards that minimize the number of false positives in partial match searches. This would prevent individuals in the DNA database from being erroneously targeted as relatives of an unknown offender, which would in turn shield their relatives from unwarranted intrusions. Another recommendation is to limit the technique's use to investigations involving the most serious crimes. Policy-makers could also require forensic laboratories to destroy genetic samples linked to exonerated suspects, and they could prohibit laboratories from conducting genetic analyses that y field information related to a person's health and behavior. They could prohibit law enforcement officials from disclosing information that will contradict family beliefs about their biological relatedness, too. Last, policy-makers could require police departments to study the effectiveness of familial identification over time, to determine its actual value in solving crimes.

Familial DNA identification's disproportionate impact on African Americans and Latinos remains a serious problem. Some scholars are so disturbed by this problem that they endorse a radical remedy: a forensic DNA database containing genetic profiles of everyone in the country. (8) Such a drastic step would eliminate the need for familial DNA identification, but it would expose everyone to significant privacy intrusions. Widespread support for this step seems unlikely in the United States, where liberty and privacy are so highly valued. In the meantime, however, familial DNA identification could exacerbate racial inequities in the law enforcement system.

Acknowledgments

I am grateful to Sonia Suter for comments on an earlier draft of this column.

(1.) For information about the case, see M. Dolan, J. Rubin, and M. Landsberg, "DNA Leads to Arrest in Grim Sleeper Killings," Los Angeles Times, July 8, 2010; "Grim Sleeper," Wikipedia, http://en.wikipedia.org/wiki/Grim_Sleeper (accessed November 30, 2010).

(2.) California Department of Justice, "DNA Partial Match (Crime Scene DNA Profile to Offender) Policy," Information Bulletin No. 2008-BFS-01, http://ag.ca.gov/cms_attachments/press/pdfs/n1548_08-bfs-01.pdf.

(3.) See N. Ram, "DNA Confidential: State Law Enforcement Policies for Genetic Databases Lack Transparency," http://scienceprogress.org/2009/11/dna-confidential.

(4.) See S. Suter, "All in the Family: Privacy and DNA Familial Searching," Harvard Journal of Law and Technology 3 (2010): 309-99, at 372-73.

(5.) Ibid., 370.

(6.) See H. Greely et al., "Family Ties: The Use of DNA Offender Databases to Catch Offenders' Kin," Journal of Law, Medicine and Ethics 34 (2006): 248-62.

(7.) Suter, "All in the Family," 352-62.

(8.) See D. Kaye and M. Smith, "DNA Identification Databases: Legality, Legitimacy, and the Case for Population-Wide Coverage," Wisconsin Law Review (2003): 413-59.

13

Crime Scene, DNA Focus of Testimony in Murder Trial

Holly Herman

June 01--Kathy A. Leibig's blood was found on a gray sweat shirt worn by the Reading man accused of fatally stabbing her, a state police forensic scientist testified Tuesday in Berks County Court. Robert M. Bonczek's account of his analysis of evidence collected in Leibig's homicide case highlighted the fourth day of testimony in Glenn Lyons' first-degree murder trial before Judge Paul M. Yatron. Leibig was found stabbed 36 times in her sport utility vehicle on the grounds of Wernersville State Hospital, South Heidelberg Township, in May 2008.

But before Bonczek took the stand, a series of troopers explained how police found Lyons' bloody sweat shirt after three days of searching trash in a recycling center in Lebanon. Bonczek said the person who was wearing the gray sweat shirt was a maximum of 3 feet away from Leibig when she was stabbed. Bonczek testified that Leibig's body was found in the back seat of her SUV with a bloody green T-shirt, jeans and undergarments. Last week, state troopers testified that Lyons, who was having an affair with Leibig, told them that men in yellow-hooded sweat shirts knocked him out when he was with Leibig in her car. They

---

Source: Crime Scene, DNA focus of testimony in murder trial. Reading Eagle, June 1, 2011. Reprinted by permission of Reading Eagle Company.

testified that Lyons said he was upset his girlfriend was killed, and another witness said last week that Lyons told him he performed CPR on Leibig. "Was there any evidence to show that Kathy Leibig was hugged after she was robbed and murdered?" Assistant District Attorney Jonathan H. Kurland asked. "No," Bonczek said.

Bonczek also said two broken knives were found in the back seat of the SUV. He said it appears Leibig tried to get to the front seat of the SUV. "She was found in the rear-passenger part of the vehicle with her body facing forward," Bonczek said. Bonczek refuted Lyons' statement to police about the men in yellow sweat shirts breaking in the car. "The lack of blood in the jams of the back doors indicated that the doors were closed during this blood-shedding incident," Bonczek testified. Under cross-examination by Lyons' lawyer, Assistant Public Defender Timothy A. Biltcliff, Bonczek said Leibig's fingernails were not tested because of a backlog of forensic evidence in other cases. Bonczek said the result would likely be that Leibig's own blood would be found under her nails. Police said the two knives found in the SUV matched a knife that was found in Lyons' apartment.

Witnesses testified last week that Lyons went on a three-day cocaine binge with people he met in Lebanon after the slaying. Timothy Seigrist, owner of Lebanon United Jobbers, a wholesale store, testified that he saw a video recorded at the parking lot of his store that shows three men jumping out of a car in an alley near the trash recycling area. Witnesses said the trash goes from a bin at Jobbers to Brandywine Recyclers Center Inc. in Lebanon. State police Cpl. William Volchko testified that police found a bag containing the bloody sweat shirt and Leibig's purse after searching the trash for three days at Brandywine Recycling. Prosecution witnesses are expected to continue testifying today. Contact Holly Herman: 610-478-6291 or hherman@readingeagle.com.

14

When DNA Evidence Suggests 'Innocent,' Some Prosecutors Cling to 'Maybe"

Erica Goode

For 17 years, Terrill Swift and three other men convicted in the 1994 rape and strangulation of a prostitute here have insisted on their innocence. And last May, a powerful new piece of evidence emerged that appeared to back their claim: a DNA profile, constructed from semen found in the victim's body, matched a man who was convicted of raping and strangling another prostitute a few years later.

"It's over," Mr. Swift remembers thinking when the DNA match surfaced. But six months later, the exoneration of the four men, who as teenagers confessed during questioning by the police, is still uncertain.

The Cook County state's attorney has opposed vacating the men's convictions, arguing that the DNA match alone is not sufficient to cast significant doubt on their guilt. Johnny Douglas, whose DNA matched the profile, was known to frequent prostitutes and could have had

Source: When DNA evidence suggest 'innocent', some prosecutors cling to 'maybe'. The New York Times, November 16, 2011, pA19.

consensual sex with the victim before the murder occurred, the prosecutors have argued.

Defense lawyers and some criminal justice experts say that the case illustrates the resistance mounted by a minority of prosecutors around the country in the face of exculpatory DNA evidence. On Wednesday, a Cook County circuit court judge is expected to rule on whether the convictions of the four men, two of whom are still in prison, should be dismissed.

Hundreds of people in the United States have been cleared by DNA evidence over the last two decades, in some cases after confessing to crimes, often in great detail. Juveniles, researchers have found, are more likely to make false confessions. Four of the five teenagers who were convicted in the brutal 1989 rape of Trisha Meili, known as the Central Park jogger, for example, confessed to the rape but were later exonerated when DNA evidence confirmed another man's involvement.

For most prosecutors, the presence of post-conviction DNA evidence is enough to prompt action. An examination of 194 DNA exonerations found that 88 percent of the prosecutors joined defense lawyers in moving to vacate the convictions. But in 12 percent of the cases, the prosecutors opposed the motions, and in 4 percent, they did so even after a DNA match to another suspect.

Brandon L. Garrett, a professor of law at the University of Virginia, who studied the exonerations last year, said that many of the cases in which prosecutors dispute the significance of DNA evidence involve defendants who initially confessed to the crimes.

In the Chicago case, said Joshua Tepfer, a lawyer at Northwestern's Center on Wrongful Convictions of Youth, who represents Mr. Swift, "there has never been a stronger hit in the DNA area."

Mr. Tepfer noted that Mr. Douglas, who was in the neighborhood when the body was found and was interviewed by the police at the time, "preyed on at-risk women, on prostitutes, and he engaged in sex and strangled them to death. It's just an identical situation."

But Anita Alvarez, the state's attorney, said a DNA match was not automatically cause for dismissal of the convictions. "DNA evidence in and of itself is not always the 'silver bullet' that it is sometimes perceived to be," Ms. Alvarez said.

Mr. Douglas, she said, who was shot to death in 2008, was "the type of person that was utilizing prostitutes. He didn't kill every other prostitute he was with."

"As a prosecutor, I have a duty to the victims in this case," she said. "I have a duty to look at everything and weigh it."

Mr. Swift, now 34 and on parole, said his own confession came out of terror and exhaustion after being questioned for hours by the police, who told him, he said, that if he worked with them and signed the confession he could go home but if not, he would go to prison for the rest of his life.

"I was 17, I'd never been in any type of trouble like that," he said. "I didn't know the weight or the magnitude of what a confession could do. It cost me 17 years of my life."

Mr. Swift said that he had not known Nina Glover, the prostitute whose brutalized body was found in a Dumpster behind a building in the South Side's Englewood neighborhood on Nov. 7, 1994, and that he had been only slightly acquainted with the four other young men who became his co-defendants. Pulled in for questioning four months after the murder, each gave graphic accounts of the rape and murder, but differed on details like the order in which they raped Ms. Glover and how many youths were involved.

Mr. Swift, prosecutors say, also pointed out a spot in a lagoon in nearby Sherman Park, where the police said they had found a shovel and mop handle used to beat Ms. Glover before she was strangled. Mr. Swift said that the police told him that the tools had been tossed into the lagoon and took him there, and that he had just pointed in a general direction at the water. The lagoon, he said, is a dumping ground for trash of all types.

Investigators found semen in Ms. Glover's vagina, but DNA testing conducted at the time excluded all five defendants and no other forensic evidence connected them to the crime. Still, three of the teenagers -- Mr. Swift, Michael Saunders and Harold Richardson -- were convicted at trial and received sentences of 30 to 40 years in prison, and the fourth, Vincent Thames, pleaded guilty. The fifth young man, Jerry Fincher, was initially charged but a judge suppressed his confession and he was not prosecuted.

Peter Neufeld, co-director of the Innocence Project and a lawyer for Mr. Saunders, who remains in prison, said that the new DNA evidence pointing to Mr. Douglas, who pleaded guilty to the 1997 rape and murder of a woman with whom he traded cocaine for sex and who was suspected of other violent assaults -- was more than enough to raise reasonable doubt in the minds of jurors and meet the standard for a conviction to be vacated.

This month, Ms. Alvarez moved to vacate the convictions in a case involving the 1991 rape and murder of a 14-year old girl. That case also involved five defendants, known as the Dixmoor Five, who confessed to the crime and were excluded by DNA testing at the time.

But the two murders, Ms. Alvarez said, "are not cookie-cutter type cases" and she has no plans to dismiss the convictions in the Englewood case before the judge's ruling on Wednesday.

Mr. Swift, who is living with his mother and sister in a Chicago suburb, wears an ankle monitor and has to register as a sex offender, a label that he said "hurts me more than the 15 years I did."

But on Wednesday, he hopes, he might be given a chance to get on with his life.

"It was a tragedy for everybody," he said. "We're innocent, but they didn't want to listen. But they're going to listen now. I truly believe that. I think they will."

15

Excellence in Policing Award for Forensic DNA Convictions

Applied DNA Sciences, Inc. (OTCBB: APDN), a provider of DNA-based security solutions, announced that in partnership with the Lancashire Constabulary it has received the Excellence in Policing Award which will be presented at the National Policing Improvement Agency's conference centre at Ryton-on-Dunsmore on September 21, 2010. This award is designed to promote the sharing of creative and innovative projects that are enhancing performance and productivity for the overall benefit of the UK police.

Neil Hunter, Lancashire Constabulary Detective Superintendant, commented, "This is a testament to the groundbreaking forensic work with Applied DNA Sciences that inextricably linked the criminals to the DNA evidence recovered. We continue to work hard to catch and convict cash-in-transit criminals who have been marked with SigNature(R) DNA."

Richard "Bo" Dietl, Chairman of Beau Dietl & Associates, a noted Security and Investigative Firm, stated, "ACPO's recognition of Excellence in Policing for the joint forensic and intelligence work conducted by Applied DNA Sciences and the Lancashire Police represents a smarter way of deterring cash crimes. DNA is the only true

Source: Excellence in Policing Award for Forensic DNA Convictions. Stony Brook, N.Y., August 5, 2010. Copyright 2010. Applied DNA Sciences, Inc. All rights reserved.

forensic marker that can help to put criminals away for a long time. This technology that Applied DNA Sciences brings to the table enhances the ability of law enforcement agencies, at home as well as on a global scale, to combat these crimes that are rapidly increasing. In all of my years in law enforcement and the private sector, I have not come across a finer forensic security solution that can be used in conjunction with law enforcement for successful prosecutions of these criminals."

In 2009, GBP 17.1m was stolen during 1,060 CViT (Cash-and-Valuables-in-Transit) robberies in the UK which accounts for 75.5% of all CViT robberies globally. In December 2008, a CViT robbery occurred in Lancashire, where a Loomis security van was attacked and a security guard was shot. The award was given for both parties' involvement in securing the convictions of the criminals who shot and wounded the security guard during that robbery.

It is believed that the opportunity to aggressively market this success will act as a significant crime deterrent to others considering such offenses. All the police agencies involved in this partnership are committed to continuing this collaboration.

"The arsenal of forensic DNA capabilities that are being used on a daily basis should send a very strong message to criminals -- if you rob Loomis, you will get caught and go to jail for a long time. We have access to an entire network comprising police and forensic CSI, and now cutting edge DNA technologies that can link individuals or organized groups to cash crimes committed. Our Zero Tolerance program is clearly removing the criminal element from the streets and keeping our employees and the general public safe," stated Tony Benson, Risk Director, Loomis UK.

APDN provides the CViT industry with its SigNature DNA, which is placed with cash staining dye into CViT boxes at the time of commissioning. The Lancashire CViT robbery involved a Loomis cash box. The information content of the encrypted DNA absolutely identifies the attached box and the date/time of the crime can be determined from the box itself.

After marketing this protocol within the CViT industry, APDN began to receive cases from UK police forces. The primary objective and benchmark of the success of this partnership has always been measured against the successful:

1. identification of APDN SigNature DNA on submitted evidence linking the evidence to reported CViT crimes, 2. presentation of that evidence at court leading to convictions, 3. prosecution and conviction and sentencing of the CViT criminal, 4. reduction of CViT offenses.

According to Dr. James A. Hayward, CEO of APDN, "We have successfully authenticated evidence in thirty-five different cases from multiple UK Police forces and have achieved a 100% success rate in linking submissions to dye stained stolen CViT. This has resulted in thirteen individuals being convicted of offenses with three more cases still awaiting trial. In the Lancashire investigation during which the security guard was shot, five defendants were convicted and jailed for over sixty years. In another case, APDN and the police were able to link together a series of twenty-three robberies in which over GBP 300,000 was stolen, based on DNA authentication. As a direct result of these authentications, these individuals have been sentenced to terms of imprisonment from between eighteen months up to life imprisonment. The total aggregate years in prison is in excess of one hundred years. All told, APDN's customers enjoyed a 49% reduction in losses as a result of CViT offenses year-to-year while the UK industry as a whole saw a decrease in losses of only 34%."

ABOUT APDN

APDN sells patented DNA security solutions to protect products, brands and intellectual property from counterfeiting and diversion. SigNature DNA is a botanical mark used to authenticate products in a unique manner that essentially cannot be copied. APDN also provides BioMaterial GenoTyping(TM) by detecting genomic DNA in natural materials to authenticate finished products. Both technologies protect brands and products in a wide range of industries and provide a forensic chain of evidence that can be used to prosecute perpetrators. To learn more, go to (www.adnas.com).

The statements made by APDN may be forward-looking in nature and are made pursuant to the safe harbor provisions of the Private Securities Litigation Reform Act of 1995. Forward-looking statements describe APDN's future plans, projections, strategies and expectations, and are based on assumptions and involve a number of risks and uncertainties, many of which are beyond the control of APDN. Actual results could differ materially from those projected due to our short operating history, limited financial resources, limited market acceptance, market competition and various other factors detailed from time to time in APDN's SEC reports and filings, including our Annual Report on Form 10-K, filed on December 23, 2009 and our subsequent quarterly reports on Form 10-Q. APDN undertakes no obligation to update publicly any forward-looking statements to reflect new information, events or circumstances after the date hereof to reflect the occurrence of unanticipated events.

16

Forensic DNA Shown to Lower Crime Rates and Decrease Property Loss

Applied Biosystems, a division of Life Technologies (NASDAQ:LIFE), announced that its forensic DNA solutions are successfully being used for a broader range of criminal investigations that include non-violent crimes, such as burglaries, auto thefts and other property crimes. These technologies are assisting law enforcement agencies, such as the Denver Crime Laboratory Bureau to reduce property crimes by more than 30%, saving more than $5 million in police costs and preventing an estimated $36.8 million of property loss during the past three years (see also Applied Biosystems).

By using forensic DNA solutions for non-violent crimes, the Denver Crime Laboratory Bureau reported doubling the identification of suspects as well as successfully prosecuting twice as many property crime cases.

Property crimes are one of the most significant economic issues in the United States, accounting for $17.6 billion in financial losses for property owners in 2007, according to FBI statistics. Of those cases, less than 17% were actually solved. Applying forensic DNA to

Source: Forensic DNA Shown to Lower Crime Rates and Decrease Property Loss, Carlsbad, CA., February 19, 2009. Copyright 2009. Life Technologies Corporation. All rights reserved.

investigate these crimes is an emerging best practice for law enforcement that is being employed in Denver and other municipalities.

"The power of forensic DNA to solve violent crimes has been well documented over the past several years," said Sonny Jackson, Public Information Officer for the Denver Police Department. "We see forensic DNA as a great tool that allows us to look at all facets of crime, including property crimes."

Recent advancements by Applied Biosystems have made the processing of DNA evidence more streamlined and accelerated, allowing more widespread use of this powerful technology. This includes automating routine DNA analysis and providing computerized forensic expert software systems that facilitate more efficient manual review of complex samples. These new tools are enabling higher productivity in forensic laboratories, leading to faster analysis and more cost-effective investigations.

"Streamlining forensic DNA testing is enabling law enforcement agencies to apply this powerful technology that was once reserved almost exclusively for violent crimes to a broader range of case work evidence," said Leonard Klevan, Ph.D., Division President of Applied BiosystemsE Applied Markets business. "The power of this technology in helping to prosecute as well as prevent crimes in Denver can be successfully replicated elsewhere, as we continue to make 21st-century forensic technologies accessible to agencies and laboratories around the world."

Applied Biosystems is a global leader in providing innovative instrument systems to accelerate academic and clinical research, drug discovery and development, pathogen detection and forensic DNA analysis. It is a market leader in forensic DNA solutions that include genetic analyzers, reagent kits, PCR and Real-Time PCR systems and software applications. Applied Biosystems, along with Invitrogen u a leading provider of platform independent, essential life science technologies for disease and drug research, bioproduction and diagnostics u is part of Life Technologies. Together, Applied Biosystems and Invitrogen provide the broadest portfolio of forensic DNA technologies available from a single company. Applied Biosystems and Invitrogen products are used in nearly every major laboratory in the world.

For more information, please visit: www.appliedbiosystems.com and www.invitrogen.com. Additional resources about forensic science can also be found at www.aafs.org. About Life Technologies Life Technologies Corporation (NASDAQ:LIFE) is a global biotechnology tools company dedicated to improving the human condition. Our systems, consumables and services enable researchers to accelerate scientific exploration, driving to discoveries and developments that make life even better. Life Technologies customers do their work across the biological spectrum, working to advance personalized medicine, regenerative science, molecular diagnostics, agricultural and environmental research, and 21st century forensics. Life Technologies had sales of more than $3 billion in 2008, employs approximately 9,500 people, has a presence in more than 100 countries, and possesses a rapidly growing intellectual property estate of approximately 3,600 patents and exclusive licenses. Life Technologies was created by the combination of Invitrogen Corporation and Applied Biosystems Inc. For more information on how we are making a difference please visit our website: www.lifetechnologies.com. Copyright 2009. Life Technologies Corporation. All rights reserved.

This article was prepared by Biotech Week editors from staff and other reports. Copyright 2009, Biotech Week via NewsRx.com.

17

Unmasking Scientific Controversies
Forensic DNA Analysis in Canadian Legal Cases of Sexual Assault

Andrea Quinlan; Curtis Fogel; Elizabeth Quinlan

Since the late 1980s, forensic DNA analysis has became a central practice within the legal response to sexual violence in Canada. DNA analysis is used in these cases to scientifically demonstrate the occurrence of a sexually violent act and to identify its perpetrator (Nelkin and Lindee). Although DNA analysis has aided in the successful resolution of some Canadian sexual assault cases, as defined by the conviction of a sexual assault offender (Gerlach), there continues to be a need for critical feminist reflection on the efficacy of DNA analysis in legal cases of sexual assault.

Despite the increasing use of DNA analysis in the Canadian legal system, much of its history and current uses and procedures have remained largely invisible to the public. Although the history of DNA analysis in sexual assault cases has been relatively short, it has been riddled with controversy, from Canadian feminists arguing for more systematic procedures in the legal handling of sexual assault to scientific communities debating the validity and reliability of different

Source: Unmasking scientific controversies: forensic DNA analysis in Canadian legal cases of sexual assault by Andrea Quinlan, Curtis Fogel, Elizabeth Quinlan. Canadian Woman Studies, Fall 2009, v28il p98(10).

approaches to DNA analysis. These historical and contemporary debates around DNA analysis have remained absent from public discourse. The contemporary scientific practices involved in DNA analysis have been similarly made invisible to victims (1) of violence and their communities of support. Despite the significant impact these practices have on the lives of victims and their communities, they are often encased in legal and scientific discourses that render them inaccessible. This paper tackles the invisibility that surrounds forensic DNA analysis in cases of sexual assault in an effort to enliven feminist reflection on the scientific practices involved in the legal response to sexual violence.

Few academic works have outlined the debates and contentious issues among feminists, scientists, and legal professionals regarding the nature and use of DNA analysis in cases of sexual violence. This paper addresses this gap by first outlining some of the historical controversy surrounding DNA analysis in the Canadian legal system. It then turns to a discussion of some of the current debates within the scientific community regarding the appropriate technologies for DNA analysis.

This paper will conclude with a critical discussion of DNA analysis in cases of sexual assault and raise a call to feminist thinkers to address the question: what are the consequences for Canadian women of DNA analysis in the legal handling of sexual violence? The authors of this paper recognize that not all women share the same lived experiences of sexual violence and the Canadian legal system. However, there is a significant lack of empirical research on the experiences of women, particularly racialized women, in relation to the collection and analysis of DNA evidence. For the purposes of this preliminary investigation of the area, this paper assumes some shared experiences between women in relation to forensic science in cases of sexual assault, and uses the singular term woman to reflect this assumption.

Before beginning this discussion, two central concepts important to this paper will be outlined for those unfamiliar with the scientific practices involved in the legal handling of cases of sexual assault in Canada. These concepts are DNA and the Sexual Assault Evidence Kit (SAEK).

DNA (DEOXYRIBONUCLEIC ACID)

DNA is an abbreviation for deoxyri- bonucleic acid. This specific nucleic acid has been suggested to be the "blueprint of the body", or the map of an individual's genetic information (Solicitor General of Canada 2). Individuals are considered to have unique DNA profiles. As such, if an individual's DNA profile can be located, it is assumed that it can be used for identification purposes. Forensic DNA analysis involves the extraction of DNA profiles from forensic samples gathered at a crime scene (Caddy and Cobb). In cases of sexual violence, the DNA profile that is generated from forensic samples is used to identify the perpetrator of the crime.

Several technologies for DNA analysis exist. The specifics of some of these methods will be discussed in this paper (Gerlach; Quinlan; Lynch; Cole, McNally and Jordan).

SEXUAL ASSAULT EVIDENCE KIT

The Sexual Assault Evidence Kit (SAEK) (2) is a tool that is used in the medical examinations of victims of sexual violence. This kit is also commonly referred to as a "rape kit." (3) The SAEK contains materials, such as swabs, vials, and hair combs, which assist in the collection of various types of forensic evidence from the victim's body. The administration of the SAEK kit is completed by a trained forensic nurse and takes approximately four hours to complete (Du Mont and Parnis). During this time biological materials are extracted, and victim's injuries, emotional status, and medical and assault history are documented (Parnis and Du Mont 2002). The SAEK, once completed, is sent to the forensic laboratory. The contents of the kit are examined by forensic scientists and used to locate a potential DNA profile that could identify the perpetrator.

The SAEK and the scientific procedures that accompany its use are considered by the legal system to result in reliable, valid accounts of sexual violence. The importance placed on the SAEK within the legal institution often results in "the evidence generated through the rape kit becom[ing] the basis on which a sexual assault is deemed to have or have not occurred" (Temkin cited in Du Mont and Parnis 2003: 173). The evidence produced by the SAEK is considered scientifically sound and, thus, has equal if not silencing authority over all other voices within the court room. As Du Mont and Parnis state, the SAEK is the "tool that science converges with the law in the attempt to determine the 'truths' of women's claims of sexual violence" (2003: 847).

As will be further explored in this paper, feminist scholars and activists have criticized the use of the kit for its revictimizing effect on victims (Du Mont and Parnis, 2003; Doe, 2008). Doe states that all of the women she interviewed described the process as "painful, humiliating, intrusive and/ or a violation--a veritable second assault" (2008: 10). In addition to these critiques, feminists have called attention to the lack of standardization in the application of the SAEK across regional and provincial borders (Parnis and Du Mont 2002; Doe, 2008). This paper will trace some of these debates, while situating them within a historical narrative of DNAanalysis in Canada.

THE HISTORY OF DNA ANALYSIS IN CANADA

Despite the growing predominance of DNA analysis in the Canadian legal system, the history of controversy surrounding its use in cases of sexual assault is largely unknown. Contentious historical issues related to DNA analysis are rarely discussed in the media and are often rendered absent by forensic scientists and legal professionals. The presumed success of DNA analysis, a practice that has become tightly woven into networks of legal institutional action, conceals and masks its own historical complexity. An exploration of this complexity, however, is crucial to the project of understanding how this practice is organized in the contemporary legal system. This exploration also serves the political purpose of rendering some of these debates visible.

The use of DNA analysis in legal cases of sexual violence has a short but complex history filled with the competing voices of scientists, feminists, and legal professionals. Alec Jeffreys, a prominent British geneticist working in the 1980s, is considered by the scientific community to be responsible for the discovery forensic of DNA testing (Bieber; Gerlach). While forensic analysis stems back to the 1800s with the investigation of fingerprint evidence, Jeffreys's work marked the first exploration of forensic analysis of DNA in criminal investigations (National DNA Databank). Jeffreys and his team of scientists at the University of Leicester explored how genetic codes, considered to be reflective of an individual's genetic composition, could be extracted from cellular material (Gerlach). The team examined how an individual's genetic map remains consistent across many different types of cells in the body. In addition, the team investigated the degradation of DNA within old samples of blood and semen (Gerlach). The findings from this exploratory work formed the basis upon which DNA analysis was soon used in legal systems in North America and Western Europe.

In 1983, following several publications of Jefferys' work, a young woman in a town near Liechester in the United Kingdom was sexually assaulted and murdered (National DNA Databank). The case remained unsolved until several years later when, following a second murder, police sent a collection of blood samples from the crime scenes to Dr. Alec Jeffreys. He compared the DNA collected at each crime scene and concluded that it originated from the same individual. Blood samples from 4,500 men were collected from nearby communities until a profile that matched those round was discovered (Bieber). The man whose DNA profile matched those round at the crime scenes was convicted of two crimes: murder and sexual assault.

THE HISTORY OF THE SEXUAL ASSAULT EVIDENCE KIT

Alongside these scientific developments in the 1980s in the United Kingdom, feminist groups in Canada were lobbying for the improvement of medical and legal responses to sexual violence (Feldberg). In 1978, the Ontario Provincial Secretariat for Justice held a consultation on tape where lawyers, police officers, rape crisis professionals, and physicians met to discuss the issues surrounding the medical care of victims of sexual assault and the gathering of forensic evidence (Feldberg). Unlike its contemporary use, forensic evidence in the early 1980s was not collected for the purposes of DNA analysis. Physical evidence was instead used to determine if male sperm was present on a woman's body and if a physical struggle between the victim and perpetrator had occurred. Things such as clothing, hair, and blood samples were collected for analysis (National DNA Databank). While the analysis of physical evidence was routinely used in legal cases of sexual violence, its impact and usefulness has been widely debated (Feldberg; Martin et al.).

Feminist groups and several other professionals argued that the lack of standardization in the collection of forensic evidence rendered the results of its analysis problematic (Parnis and Du Mont 2006). The tension at the time was described in the following lines:

Community-based feminists, crisis workers and some medical, scientific, law enforcement and legal professionals complained that inadequate and haphazard medical and forensic evidence collection practices were meeting neither the needs of sexually assaulted women nor those of the legal system with respect to providing reliable and useful evidence. (Parnis and Du Mont 2006: 77)

As a result of pressure from these feminist groups, the consultation on rape developed the Sexual Assault Evidence Kit (SAEK). The current SAEK contains materials to assist in the collection of forensic evidence, including, "cotton swabs, test tubes, microscope slides, a comb and fingernail dippers" (Martin et al.). The swabs, test tubes, and microscope slides were designed to collect semen and blood, and fingernail clippers for collecting fingernails if the victim scratched the assailant (Martin et al.). While the formation of the SAEK calmed some of the debate regarding forensic evidence collection in cases of sexual assault, new controversies regarding its production and use emerged.

DNA ANALYSIS IN CANADA

In 1989, the RCMP employed DNA analysis for the first time in a sexual assault case that occurred in Ottawa (RCMP 2003). Reports have suggested that Hilary McCormack, the Crown prosecutor of the case, was familiar with some of the developments in DNA analysis that were forming in the United States. She had reportedly planned to send forensic samples from the case to the newly formed private DNA labs across the border. However, before the samples were sent, the RCMP made an offer to conduct the analysis locally (RCMP 2003). As McCormack remembers, "it was going to be far less expensive and would also give the RCMP an opportunity to enhance their knowledge and expertise in this new field" (McCormack cited in RCMP 2003: 13).

Following in the path of Jefferys' work, a DNA code of the perpetrator was extracted from the forensic samples and was then compared to the DNA of the suspect. When a match was found, it was concluded that the suspect was the perpetrator (National DNA Bank). While the victim of the case had previously visually identified the perpetrator, the suspect had denied any involvement with the crime (National DNA Bank). The scientific findings, however, significantly altered the course of the trial. During the court case, the suspect changed his plea to guilty. The case set a historical precedent as it marked the first time

DNA analysis was conducted by the RCMP for its successful use in a Canadian legal case.

After the success of the 1989 trial, DNA analysis became a common, although not uncontested, practice in the legal system. As Neil Gerlach contends, DNA testing formed the "new forensic paradigm with tremendous authority" (38). The SAEK became the tool through which forensic samples were collected from the woman's body, and DNA analysis the instrument that uncovered the facts of rape. Feldberg describes the kit of the 1990s by stating,

> In a society where hard facts and scientific truths are revered, the purpose of the kit is to provide corroboration in the form of meticulous scientific evidence ... it attempts to produce "hard" physical evidence that will withstand scrutiny better than more subjective emotional/psychological measures. (110)

With the influx of DNA analysis into the legal system, the voice of science came to dominate the courtrooms of sexual violence cases. Victims' stories of violence became overshadowed by the authoritative claims of forensic science (Quinlan). Despite DNA's appearance of authority in the Canadian courtroom, various feminists, scientists, and legal professionals have debated the terms of its use. The debates have helped to expose the unfounded assumption that DNA analysis works in victims' best interests. In doing so, these debates have not only charted out crucial beginnings to a feminist critique of DNA evidence in sexual assault cases, but have also laid the groundwork for possible future analyses of the sexist and racist views of female sexuality and racialized women that accompany the introduction of forensic science in the courtroom. While the influence of racism on women's experiences of reporting sexual assault has been empirically taken up by some (Doe 2009), the intersection of racism and DNA analysis in sexual assault cases appears significantly understudied. There is a need for further empirical and theoretical work in this area.

This paper will focus on some of the contentions that feminist scholars and grassroots activists raised in relation to DNA evidence in cases of sexual assault.

DNA Analysis in the 1990s

In 1996, the Solicitor General of Canada spoke to the new found power of DNA analysis by stating: "DNA can focus investigations, and will likely shorten trials and lead to guilty pleas. It could also deter some offenders from committing serious offences. The increased use of forensic DNA evidence will lead to longterm saving for the criminal justice system" (2). While DNA typing was regarded by some to be the technology that was going to revolutionize the legal system, others raised strong reservations surrounding its use.

Patricia Lee, a grassroots feminist working at a Vancouver Rape Relief Centre, placed the presumed power of DNA analysis in a new light. She argued that the authority DNA was gaining in the legal system, as well as within broader society, could be detrimental to the interests of female victims of sexual violence. She claimed that:

> In the few sexual assault cases where DNA evidence could be useful, it seems likely that attackers who realize the strength of the scientific evidence against them will switch from "identity" to "consent" as their defense. This means that instead of claiming that he was not the man who attacked her, the accused will claim that she agreed to sexual contact. It has already been demonstrated in Canadian courts that consent cases are harder to win. This could mean that with increased use of DNA technology, the conviction rate will not increase, and may even decrease. (2)

This argument, as well as the many others that echoed its sentiment, was in sharp contradiction to that of the Solicitor General's contention that DNA analysis would be the new time-saving device of the legal system.

Despite this dispute, and many others of its kind, DNA analysis grew to become a central practice in the Canadian legal system (Gerlach). The RCMP Forensics Division expanded to allow for the influx of forensic samples that required testing, and forensic experts were routinely brought into the courtroom to explain their findings. This increased presence of science in the courtroom brought further critiques.

Silencing Women's Voices

Feminists in the 1990s argued that the authority of forensic science in the courtroom worked to silence women's voices and their narratives of sexual violence (Feldberg). Julie Kubanek and Fiona Miller asserted that the introduction of DNA evidence brought with it an increased reliance on scientific expertise (Kubanek and Miller). They stated that, "in the eyes of the judge and jurors, the verbal testimony of ... the victim, cannot carry the statistical reliability of scientific evidence, a bias which can only work against women in the majority of cases" (3). In Kubanek and Miller's analysis, women and their experiences were overshadowed by the imposition of DNA in the legal system. Echoing this contention, Georgina Feldberg quotes a victim of rape who reflected on her experience within the courtroom: "'I felt like an exhibit at my own trial; I had no voice, the experts and facts spoke instead of me'" (113).

Feminists like Kubanek, Miller, and Feldberg claimed that despite the 1979 attempts to remedy the institutional handling of sexualized violence, the influx of DNA analysis served to reinforce and recreate traditional power inequalities between victims of violence and the legal system. As Feldberg argued, "the path to reform has led us onto troubled ground, and in some respects, the very tools we developed to achieve reform have in fact inhibited it" (110).

THE AUTHORITY OF FORENSIC SCIENCE

Throughout its short history, the voice of forensic science has carried with it the authority of being the "heroic truth" within legal cases of sexual violence (Di Fonzo). As J. Herbie DiFonzo suggests, since its inception "DNA forensic procedures have attained the courtroom air of flawlessness, often referred to as the 'mystical spell' of DNA" (2). Along a similar vein, the RCMP National DNA Data Bank Annual Report states that DNA analysis marks the "dawn of a new era in the administration of justice in Canada ... our work provides safer streets and safer communities for all Canadians and increasingly, for citizens around the world" (5). From all appearances, DNA analysis has grown to become a stable, uncontested practice within the legal system. However, it can be argued that this stability is an illusion.

Despite the growing reliance on DNA analysis in the Canadian legal system, many debates surrounding its use have continued. Feminists since the 1990s have continued to critique the ways in which the scientific voice has overpowered women's voices in the courtroom. In addition to these critiques, debate has also extended into the scientific community, where significant controversy over the technologies, procedures, and interpretations of DNA analysis in cases of sexual assault exists. While these controversies flourish between scientists and legal professionals, they often remain invisible or inaccessible to victims of violence and their support communities.

In an effort to bring some of these debates into the public eye, the following section will outline some of the contemporary scientific controversies surrounding the use of DNA analysis in cases of sexual assault. While many debates surrounding robotics and automation, standardization, and technological change exist within the scientific community studying DNA, this section will focus specifically on the controversies surrounding the privatization of DNA analysis in Canada. (4)

Contemporary Scientific Controversies: Privatizing DNA Analysis

Since the first Canadian legal case to use DNA analysis in 1989, the vast majority of forensic analysis in Canada has been conducted in publically funded Royal Canadian Mounted Police forensic labs. However, there are now approximately nine privately funded DNA labs in Canada in addition to the public RCMP forensic laboratories (Quinlan). Two of these privately funded labs are accredited (5) to do forensic DNA casework. Presently, however, the involvement of these labs in legal cases of sexual violence has been somewhat limited. To date, the private labs have been primarily involved in conducting analyses that have been contracted by the defence counsel (6) as well as secondary analyses for the RCMP. As the popularity and reputations of these labs grow, however, this limited use is beginning to change.

The methods for DNA analysis used in the RCMP and private Canadian labs are similar, but there are some notable differences. For example, one Canadian private lab, similar to the RCMP, uses what is called PCR/STR nuclear profiling (Quinlan). However, this lab also uses other technologies that have been argued by some to be more sensitive than those used by the RCMP. While most of the RCMP technologies have the ability to isolate and examine 9-13 locations on the DNA strand, methods used in the private lab have the capacity to locate 15-19 locations on the DNA strand (Quinlan). This greater number of locations has been suggested to increase the accuracy of the analysis.

While this scientific development appears as though it would have a positive effect on cases of sexual violence, the discrepancy of practices between the publicly and privately funded labs in Canada have introduced the problem of divergent scientific results, an outcome that could challenge the authority the legal system has granted forensic DNA analysis. The prospect of inconclusive or contradictory forensic results that could result from differing practices raises questions about the ability of the legal system to make use of developing science. In addition, the tensions between public and private labs introduce the possible misuse of differing scientific practices and results by the defence. While much further discussion and exploration of these developing sciences is needed, critical thinkers should consider the possible impacts of differing scientific practices.

Mitochondrial DNA

A few private DNA labs in Canada have introduced "mitochondrial DNA profiling (mtDNA)" to the Canadian scientific community (Quinlan). This approach, although similar to what is used by the RCMP, involves the analysis of different locations within the cell. Instead of examining nuclear material, mtDNA analysis focuses on the mitochondria in the cell (cellular material that is outside of the nucleus). There are 700-2000 mitochondria within a given cell (Cheng). In cases where the nuclear material of a cell is damaged or degraded, mtDNA has been suggested as being extremely effective in locating a DNA profile (Paneto et al.; Cheng). The introduction of this methodology to Canadian forensic casework by private DNA labs has raised some contentious issues.

Mitochondrial DNA testing gained its reputation for generating DNA profiles from degraded or severely damaged samples through its use in successfully identifying individuals in large mass disaster zones, such as the 2001 9/11 attack on the World Trade Centre ("DNA Missing Persons Index"). In cases of sexual violence where there is a limited amount of biological material or the material that was collected remained inside the woman's body for an extended period of time before being extracted, mtDNA has the potential to be particularly useful. Mitochondrial DNA typing has also been shown to be useful for hair analysis, more so than its nuclear DNA typing counterpart (Paneto et al.). In cases of sexual violence, where the only forensic evidence that can be gathered is a small piece of hair, mtDNA testing could also prove useful (Paneto et al.).

The exclusionary power of mtDNA is considered to be the same as methods involving the analysis of nuclear DNA (Quinlan). They can both exclude the possibility of a DNA sample being from a particular individual, when, by comparison, the DNA profiles from the two samples are round to be different. However, the "evidentiary weight" of mtDNA is thought to be different than that of nuclear DNA testing (Cheng 100). Mitochondrial DNA is inherited maternally and, as such, grandmothers, mothers, and daughters will share the same mtDNA profile. As a result, the capacity of mtDNA analysis to identify a particular individual is lessened in comparison to nuclear DNA testing. Despite this, however, mtDNA analysis has been shown to be a useful technology in some legal cases.

Public vs. Private DNA Labs: Competing Practices and Conclusions

When mtDNA was first introduced in a Canadian legal case of sexual violence, there was substantial courtroom debate regarding its validity as a method (R. v. Murrin). However, since that time, there have been several Canadian cases that have garnered much attention in the media, pointing to the increased use of private DNA labs for mtDNA analysis. While these stories are ones of legal prosecution, they introduce questions surrounding the differing practices of the public and privately funded DNA labs in Canada. The most recent case of this nature involved an unsolved murder case from 1984 that was reopened and, with the employment of mtDNA typing, was solved in 2007.

The 1984 case involved a young woman named Candace Derksen who was killed and round seven weeks later, frozen in an abandoned shed (CTV. ca). In 2001, investigators sent forensic material from the case to the RCMP laboratory for analysis. However, they were told by the RCMP that the lab was unable to process the material. The forensic samples were sent to a private Canadian DNA lab and through mitochondrial DNA testing, a profile was generated. Mark Grant, a previously convicted sexual offender, was charged on May 16, 2007 with the first-degree murder of Candace Derksen. As one Canadian reporter wrote, "Winnipeg police say they could have arrested the man accused of killing Candace Derksen more than five years ago if the National RCMP lab was able to do the [mtDNA typing] DNA testing" that was required to solve the case (Clayton).

The recent visibility of this case in the media introduces some contentious issues for DNA analysis in Canada. It marks one of the first cases in which the divergence between the methodologies employed by the RCMP and private labs in Canada was made visible to the public. However, much of the complexities of the scientific methods behind mtDNA and PCR/STR nuclear testing were not divulged in the media representations. Instead, the public was notified only of the different conclusions reached between the RCMP and private labs.

Faced with these contemporary complexities surrounding the influx of mtDNA testing in Canada, the RCMP responded in a somewhat contradictory manner. On the RCMP's website, some of the benefits of mtDNA testing are acknowledged. However, they assert that it can only serve as a "secondary analysis" as mtDNA "does not necessarily provide conclusive identification of an individual" (RCMP 2007). Further to this, a consultation paper written on the possibility of creating a new missing persons index in the Data Bank stated that "the scientific techniques required for mitochondrial DNA analysis are significantly more expensive and time consuming that those for nuclear DNA" (Public Safety and Emergency Preparedness Canada). The expense that would be required to implement a new technology in the RCMP labs would be large, which explains the RCMP's hesitation to introduce mtDNA testing (Quinlan). However, with the increased visibility of cases requiring mtDNA testing, it is possible that the RCMP may choose to implement the technology in the future. Until such time, Canadian DNA analysis will struggle with the current disjuncture between practices in the RCMP and private DNA labs.

While cases such as the Candace Derksen murder introduce some questions about the results assembled in the RCMP labs, the common practice has been to place full trust in the RCMP's conclusions (Quinlan). When the RCMP stated that no DNA could be round on the woman's body, their contention remained unchallenged until a private DNA lab with alternative technologies proved otherwise. As has been suggested in this paper, DNA analysis has been given an authoritative voice within the legal system. It is assumed that results from the forensic laboratory are "truth." Conclusions drawn in the laboratory have significant impact on victims of violence and their experiences within the legal system. As feminists concerned with enacting change in the legal institution, we should be considering the impact of these divergent scientific practices and conclusions on victims of violence, their supporting communities, and Canadian legal precedent.

FEMINIST PERSPECTIVES

The authority that DNA analysis has been granted in Canadian cases of sexual assault alongside the growing controversies in the scientific forensic community raise some significant questions for feminists. Some of these questions will be explored in this section.

The Problem of Consent

As feminists in the 1990s contended, the rise of DNA analysis in cases of sexual violence has the potential to shift legal focus from the problem of the identification of the perpetrator to the issue of proof of non-consent. The "consent defence" can be used by defence attorneys to suggest that no crime has occurred, regardless of DNA evidence revealing sexual contact. The result could be that women would be forced back into the courtroom for the purposes of being prodded and probed in attempts to reveal that they in some way consented to the activity, or at least that the accused thought she did.

Further, with the increased focus on DNA analysis in sexual assault cases, police and prosecutors may hesitate to pursue those cases where DNA cannot be obtained from the crime scene or from the woman. This result is particularly problematic where, for example, the woman has declined the SAEK to avoid being re-victimized. This presents some crucial issues for victims seeking legal resolution and feminists fighting for change in the legal system, issues that must be seriously considered.

Transparency

Gerlach suggests that with the increase in public awareness of DNA analysis and the sensationalized accounts of the technology in the media, the contemporary Canadian legal system runs the risk of attributing DNA results with more power than they deserve. He writes "judges and lawyers, and even scientists, are all too easily misled regarding the sorts of conclusions a DNA match allows them to make about the defendant's guilt or innocence" (46). The lack of transparency surrounding the controversies of DNA analysis in Canada perpetuates visions of its power and ability to uncover truth. This could have significant consequences for victims of violence, whose mistaken faith in the power of DNA evidence could lead to consenting to invasive DNA collection procedures without full knowledge of how their DNA will be used and stored, as well as the efficacy of forensic DNA testing.

In an effort to address these issues, there must be greater demand for transparency around the practices and controversies involved in DNA analysis in cases of sexual violence. The results of DNA analysis have profound impacts on the lives of countless Canadians women who experience sexual violence. The knowledge of these processes should not be restricted to the scientific community. If issues exist surrounding the effectiveness of certain methods of DNA extraction and analysis, then these issues must be openly acknowledged and represented in public discourse rather than obscured and rendered inaccessible.

The Silencing Effect

As feminists of the 1990s argued, the authority that has been granted to forensic science has worked to overshadow and, at times, silence women's experiences of sexual violence in the courtroom (Kubanek and Millet; Feldberg). Andrea Quinlan captures the voices of several Crown prosecutors who described DNA analysis as "incredibly powerful" and "the best evidence by far.... It's not an eye witness who may have had a few too many beers and might have forgotten over the past couple of months ... it's hard to explain away" (94). Statements like these speak to the way in which the scientific rendering of tape has been granted authority over all other types of evidence, including women's narration of their experience. This silencing of victims in the courtroom could lead to further trauma for reporting victims, decreased likelihood of reporting among recent victims, and increased legal and public misunderstanding of the experience of sexual violence.

The tensions in the scientific community that have been discussed in this paper may shed a new light on this discussion. The existing controversies over the conclusions of forensic science should lead to some questions about the processes that have worked to grant forensic science its authority over women's narratives within the courtroom. This paper has outlined only one of the many scientific controversies over DNA analysis. (7) As technologies continue to develop, tensions between public and private labs will grow. As feminists interested in positive change for victims in the legal system, we should be closely watching these developments in the scientific community, challenging the authority of their conclusions that have been arbitrarily granted, and demanding their greater visibility in public discourse.

CONCLUSION

As Gerlach suggests, the power we have granted DNA analysis is perhaps far more generous than it deserves. While DNA has successfully aided in the resolution of several cases, the controversies surrounding its use and the conclusions it draws should be cause for both hesitation and reflection. This paper is a starting point for further critical dialogue. It is a call to Canadian feminists to critically consider the implications of the widespread use of DNA analysis in cases of sexual assault in Canada.

Many of the cases cited in this paper were stories of successful prosecution of perpetrators. They were stories in which DNA analysis played an important role within the narrative of a completed legal case. However, this very small sampling is no t reflective of the majority of cases of sexual violence, many of which do not even make it to the courtroom. When considering the implications of a growing use of science in the legal system, we should be cognizant of the many stories that are not told, those that are ignored by popular media, and those that become stalled in the Canadian legal system, or deemed unfounded by investigators.

In the fight for progressive, positive change in the Canadian legal system, feminists, victims of violence, supportive community members, scholars, and activists should take seriously the project of interrogating the authority that science has been granted in the courtroom. We should collectively consider the implications of the invisibility of these scientific practices and controversies and jointly struggle for their transparency. In addition, we must consider ways to increase the visibility of our own critical perspectives and acknowledgment of our voices within the legal system and in public discourse.

References Omitted

(1) Within much of the feminist literature on sexual violence, the term "survivor" has been used to replace the more common term "victim". Despite this trend, there has been significant debate surrounding the meanings of these terms (McCaffrey; Lamb; Atmore; Reich; Young and Maguire). While the term victim can mistakenly suggest weakness, as some scholars have contended, it does not imply a recovered state, or even the possibility of recovery. Rather, it releases women from the societal expectation to heal, and instead acknowledges the possibility of an altered identity from which one cannot recover. Reich contends that if the term victim is to be used, it must be understood not as an encompassing identity that rigidly defines experience, but as a label that is "fluid, temporal, unstable, and complex" (16). It is in this manner that the term victim will be used throughout this work. For further discussion see Quinlan.

(2) For a narrative of the experience of the administration of the SAEK, see Doe.

(3) While the term "tape kit" is widely used in academic literature, it has been contested by some medical professionals who argue that it carries connotations with the "tools of the trade of the offender" (Crowley 104). For this reason, this work uses primarily the term Sexual Assault Evidence Kit (SAEK) to refer to the materials used in forensic medical exams.

(4) For further discussion see Quinlan.

(5) Accreditation involves "the formal, independent evaluation of a laboratory's competence to conduct specific tests" in accordance with national and international guidelines (Standards Council of Canada). Accreditation is granted to both public and private DNA labs in Canada by the Standards Council of Canada.

(6) The vast majority of DNA analysis conducted by the RCMP is done for Crown counsel. However, in some cases, the defence counsel requests expert opinion or secondary analysis. In these cases, private labs are often employed (Quinlan).

(7) Others tensions include the questionable results that have arisen from the introduction of robotics in DNA testing and analysis and the current inability of the National DNA Data Bank to store and compare

any form of DNA profile other than PCR/STR nuclear profiles. For further discussion of these scientific controversies, see Quinlan.

Andrea Quinlan is a Ph.D. student at York University. Her research interests are in the areas of the intersections between law and science, sexualized violence, and feminist theory.

Curtis Fogel is an Assistant Professor at Lakehead University, Orillia Campus in the Department of Interdisciplinary Studies. His research interests are in the area of legal issues pertaining to consent in Canada.

Elizabeth Quinlan is a faculty member at the University of Saskatchewan. Her research interests are in the areas of institutional responses to sexual assault.

Part 3

FINGERPRINT AND TRACE EVIDENCE

18

Defense Challenges Fingerprint Evidence in Murder Trial

Jamie Satterfield

The defense attorney for a man accused in a fatal shooting at a North Knoxville laundromat sparred today with an expert who said his client's fingerprints were on the driver's side door where the fatal shot was fired.

Attorney John Boucher tried to take Knoxville Police Department fingerprint expert Tim Schade to task over what he insisted is more fault-filled art than science.

Schade had testified that he identified prints left on the driver's side door of Lisa Wakefield's car as those of Jerry Romell Gray, 22, who is standing trial this week in Knox County Criminal Court in Wakefield's May 2009 slaying outside the Woodland Avenue Coin Laundry.

Boucher noted that a computer-generated list of potential print matches ranked Gray near the bottom of the list and suggested the computer was more accurate and scientific than what he termed the more subjective human analysis.

Source: Defense challenges fingerprint evidence in murder trial. Knoxville New-Sentinel, February 23, 2010.

Schade disagreed.

"The computer just gives me a list of options," he said. "I started at number one and worked my way down. I excluded all of those. It's black or white. It's either a match or it's not. It's a science."

The state has rested its case against Gray. Judge Richard Baumgartner is now giving Gray a brief break to decide if he will testify.

On Monday, jurors heard an account of the shooting from Wakefield's common law husband.

19

Maryland Judge Rubs Out Fingerprint Evidence

Carmel Sileo

A ruling in a capital murder case questions one of the most time-honored ways of figuring out whodunit.

In a Baltimore County, Maryland, courtroom, a state circuit court judge ruled that testimony about latent fingerprint evidence was not admissible because the state could not prove that it had "a reliable factual foundation." In granting the defense motion to exclude the testimony, Judge Susan Souder likened unquestioning confidence in fingerprint evidence to some people's stubborn belief in a flat Earth. (State v. Rose, No. K06-0545 (Md., Baltimore Co. Cir. Oct. 19, 2007).)

On the morning of January 5, 2006, Warren Fleming was shot to death outside a store he owned in Baltimore's Security Square Mall. Witnesses said they saw two men struggle with Fleming and then flee in a stolen car but could not identify them. When police officers recovered the car, abandoned at a subway stop, they lifted fingerprints from it and sent them to the crime lab along with the names of possible suspects. The lab technicians identified the prints as belonging to Bryan Rose. Rose was arrested and charged with Fleming's murder.

Source: Maryland judge rubs out fingerprint evidence. Carmel Sileo, Trial, Feb 2008 v44 i2 p64 (3).

The question before Souder centered on the method the technicians used, known as ACE-V (analysis, comparison, evaluation, and verification)--the most common method of identifying latent fingerprints. The defense questioned whether ACE-V was scientifically valid under the "general acceptance" standard set forth in Frye v. United States. (293 F. 1013 (D.C. Cir. 1923).) In Maryland, the standard is called Frye-Reed after the case in which the state adopted Frye. (Reed v. State, 391 A.2d 364 (Md. 1978).)

Souder wrote that the method did not meet that standard, concluding that "the proof presented by the state ... showed that it was more likely so, than not so, that ACE-V is the type of procedure Frye was intended to banish, that is, a subjective, untested, unverifiable identification procedure that purports to be infallible."

The state argued that fingerprint evidence has been accepted in courtroom testimony for over 100 years and that most courts have rejected attempts to have fingerprint evidence dismissed.

But Patrick Kent, chief attorney for the forensics division of the Maryland public defender's office, who argued the defense motion, said that was all the more reason the evidence should be challenged. "Historical acceptance is not judicial acceptance," Kent said. "There has been no meaningful litigation over this discipline for over 100 years."

Souder agreed with that view. "The state is correct that fingerprint evidence has been used in criminal cases for almost a century," she wrote. "While that fact is worthy of consideration, it does not prove reliability. For many centuries, perhaps for millennia, humans thought that the earth was flat.... Indeed, there is still a Flat Earth Society for people who cling to the idea the earth is not an orb. But science has proved that the earth is not flat; and it is the type of fact of which a court can take judicial notice."

Fingerprint evidence is so widely accepted by courts and in popular culture that it seems--and its proponents say it is--infallible. But that view has been challenged by skeptical researchers and by high-profile embarrassments: In 2004, Brandon Mayfield, a Portland, Oregon, lawyer, was arrested for the terrorist bombings on a Madrid train when the FBI concluded that his fingerprints matched those found at the crime scene. When Spanish investigators questioned the match and found a likelier suspect, Mayfield was released.

He was luckier than Stephan Cowan, a Massachusetts man who was convicted in 1997 of shooting a police officer and spent six years in prison before chance circumstances revealed that the fingerprint evidence used against him was mistaken and he was innocent.

"Most times you find out an innocent person was convicted, it's because of bad forensic evidence: eyewitness testimony, voice recognition, and fingerprint evidence," said Kent.

After the Mayfield foul-up, the FBI's Office of the Inspector General (OIG) launched an internal investigation into its fingerprint methodology. In her decision, Souder referred in detail to the OIG report, which concluded that the ACE-V produced inconsistent results.

She also cited skeptical scientific reviews of fingerprint evidence, including the work of University of California-Irvine criminologist Simon Cole, who has documented dozens of convictions based on faulty fingerprint evidence.

Souder also had harsh words for the state's expert witness, FBI fingerprints expert Stephen Meagher. "Mr. Meagher incredibly testified that there is no error rate in ACE-V as it is an infallible methodology," Souder wrote. "Mr. Meagher was neither credible nor persuasive in this regard. Without impartial testing, however, whether or not the methodology is infallible is unknown."

And contrary to Meagher's testimony, she added, "Where tests have attempted to imitate actual conditions, error rates by fingerprint examiners have been alarmingly high."

Souder's ruling raised eyebrows among defense lawyers and prosecutors across the state.

"This will turn a lot of cases on their heads," predicted Byron Warnken, a professor at the University of Baltimore School of Law. Warnken agreed that some of the protocols for ACE-V identification are "sloppy" but added that Souder erred when "she made herself the fact-finder."

"The complaints about latent fingerprinting--no standards, no independent verification, no blind review--are legitimate," Warnken said. "The problem is, these are questions that go to the weight of the evidence, not the admissibility of it. The proper way to handle this is to let the evidence in, and then let the defense minimize the weight that the jury gives to this evidence."

But Brian DeWolfe, Kent's cocounsel in the Rose hearing, said, "The judge considered that, but concluded that under Frye-Reed there has to be scientific validity before evidence can come before a fact-finder."

The judge was assuming her proper role as a "gatekeeper," said DeWolfe, who is district public defender for Montgomery County, Maryland. "Saying you have to leave it to the jury to make the determination flies in the face of the careful scrutiny that courts are required to give under Frye-Reed."

Kent said it was high time a judge realized the fallibility of this long-accepted evidence. "Anyone who wants to imbue a certain type of evidence with the power and the persuasiveness of science," he said, "must also abide by the rules of science."

20

Nature of Clothing Isn't Evidence in Rape Cases, Florida Law Says

A nationally publicized acquittal in a rape case last year has now led to a Florida law that bars rape defendants' lawyers from citing a woman's clothing as evidence justifying the attack.

A nationally publicized acquittal in a rape case last year has now led to a Florida law that bars rape defendants' lawyers from citing a woman's clothing as evidence justifying the attack.

The measure, whose sponsor calls it the first such law in the nation, was signed Friday by Gov. Bob Martinez, who said:

"There is no excuse for rape under any circumstances, and this law will make it clear that the victim of sexual battery should not be persecuted as the criminal is prosecuted. This new law is a major victory for the rights of crime victims."

JURORS HEARD OF CLOTHING

The legislation, sponsored by State Representative Elaine Gordon, Democrat of Miami, stemmed from Steven Lord's acquittal in a rape case in Fort Lauderdale last October.

Source: Nature of clothing isn't evidence in rape cases, Florida Law says. The New York Times, June 3, 1990.

Mr. Lord, 26 years old, had been accused by a woman who testified that he had abducted her at knifepoint from the parking lot of a Fort Lauderdale restaurant a year earlier and raped her repeatedly during a trip north on Interstate 95.

Several jurors interviewed after the trial said they had decided on a verdict of not guilty because at the time of the abduction, the 22-year-old woman was wearing a lace miniskirt and no underwear, evidence that had been introduced by Mr. Lord's lawyer, Tim Day. The jurors said such attire might have brought on the attack.

The acquittal brought outrage and protests from many women's groups.

Two months later, Mr. Lord pleaded guilty in Georgia to charges of kidnapping and raping a woman there. He was sentenced to a life term in prison.

CRITICISM OF LAW

The lawyer for the woman in the Fort Lauderdale case says he has found little to commend in the new law, however.

The lawyer, Alexander Siegel, termed the legislation "overkill," saying that enough rules already existed on what evidence is acceptable and that judges and lawyers should handle each case individually.

"In my opinion," he said, "the new law is unconstitutional and unnecessary. Judges are quite capable of deciding what can be introduced, and attorneys can be more aggressive about trying to keep things out."

21

Suspects Checked for Links to Other Home Invasions
Clothing, Other Evidence May Be Clues, Police Say

Nick Bonham

A top police investigator said Friday that the suspects in the recent fatal home invasion could be linked to similar crimes.

"We're certainly looking into it. Some of the descriptions match the descriptions to some of the other home invasions we've had. I know these guys were wearing masks, blue bandanas, which matches the description in other cases," said Sgt. Eric Bravo of the Pueblo Police Department.

John Pete Sullivan, 28, was killed Tuesday in the incident. Sullivan and brothers Carlos and Shane Manzanares, ages of 41 and 28, were masked and armed and tried raiding Christopher Maes' South Side home, police said. Maes, 31, shot and killed Sullivan during the incident. An autopsy confirmed Sullivan died of a single gunshot wound to the back, the coroner said Friday. The Manzanares brothers

Source: Suspects checked for links to other home invasions: Clothing, other evidence may be clues, police say. Pueblo Chieftain, May 22, 2010.

and Natasha Villalobos, 23, were arrested on warrants for first-degree burglary for their alleged roles in the crime. Villalobos, who was at the Maes' home at the time and who was reportedly dating Maes' younger brother for a short period, is believed to have planned the invasion. Villalobos and the Manzanares brothers were arrested Thursday at an apartment in Lakewood. They were staying with Missy Fuentes, 21, a niece to the brothers who was wanted for escape from Minnequa Community Corrections in Pueblo. All four suspects were still being held in the Jefferson County Detention Center on Friday waiting transfer to Pueblo.

Part 4

DETECTING LIES

22

Tessling On My Brain
The Future of Lie Detection and Brain Privacy in the Criminal Justice System

Ian Kerr; Max Binnie; Cynthia Aoki

ABSTRACT

The criminal justice system requires reliable means of detecting truth and lies. A battery of emerging neuro-imaging technologies makes it possible to gauge and monitor brain activity without the need to penetrate the cranium. Bypassing external physiological indicators of dishonesty relied upon by previous lie detection techniques, some neuro-imaging experts believe in the possibility of reliable brain-scan lie-detection systems in the criminal justice system. Because future generations of neuro-technology will become smaller and sleeker, will have greater read ranges, and could one day interface with implantable microchips, some of those experts also believe in the possibility of remote, surreptitious brain surveillance. In this article, the authors examine such possibilities and assert that Canadian courts' current approach to protecting privacy cannot easily accommodate the challenges caused by these emerging technologies. The article commences with an examination of the "reasonable expectation of

Source: Tessling on my brain: the future of lie detection and brain privacy in the criminal justice system. Ian Kerr, Max Binnie, Cynthia Aoki. Canadian Journal of Criminology and Criminal Justice, June 2008, v50 i3 p367 (21).

privacy" standard adopted by the Supreme Court of Canada, arguing that various courts across Canada have misunderstood and misapplied the R. v. Tessling decision by way of an inappropriate analogy. After a description of brain-scan lie-detection systems, the authors then examine the courts' use of the Tessling analogy in the context of brain privacy. In addition to demonstrating the danger in a generalized judicial proposition that there is no reasonable expectation of privacy in information emanating from a private place into a public space, the authors conclude that a more robust account of brain privacy is required and speculate about possible sources of law from which this might derive.

ARTICLE

When lawyers and judges describe criminal procedure, they often boil it down to two core goals: finding facts and determining guilt (Friedland and Roach 2004). Understood in this way, the criminal justice system requires reliable means of detecting truth and lies. Research indicates that the capacity for deception is to some extent biologically programmed (Lewis, Stanger, and Sullivan 1989), that it is an important stage of moral development commencing in children as early as age three (Lewis et al.), and that, as children, we learn to deceive in order to avoid punishment for acts of disobedience (Freud 1965; Spence 2001). It is therefore not surprising that lie detection has become a major preoccupation within the criminal justice system.

Although philosophers (Bok 1982; Frankfurt 2005), psychologists (Mann, Vrij, and Bull 2004), and sociologists (Barnes 1994) have appreciated the complexity of distinguishing truth from lies, our courts are increasingly looking to neuroscience as a means of reducing the search for truth to the existence or non-existence of certain brain states.

It has been said that we are entering "the golden age of neuroscience" (Bailey 2003). While neuroscience remains a nascent field of inquiry, some believe that it will one day unlock the mysteries of the human brain. Up till now, the biggest barrier has been the skull. Recently, however, a battery of new imaging technologies makes it possible to gauge and monitor brain activity without the need to penetrate the cranium (Evanson 2003). A number of emerging neuro-imaging techniques can facilitate lie detection (Ford 2006). Some allow electrical activity occurring in the brain to be measured externally and remotely. Some can even map and associate electrical activity with certain brain regions and functions.

While the spectre of intercepting brainwaves to determine whether someone is telling the truth may seem the stuff of science fiction, some courts have already adopted nascent forms of these technologies (Iowa v. Harrington). Brain scans are thought by some to have the potential to revolutionize lie detection because they bypass unreliable physiological indicators of anxiety used in older polygraph technologies, focusing instead directly on the brain states provoking those physical reactions (Appelbaum 2007). While current imaging devices are bulky, obtrusive, and conspicuous, future generations of neuro-technology promise to become smaller and sleeker. We are also told that they will have greater read ranges and could one day interface with implantable microchips (Gasson, Hutt, Goodhew, Kyberd, and Warwick 2005).

If these technologies ever live up to their hype, the possibility of remote, surreptitious brain surveillance--whether used by the police or by private actors--poses a threat to privacy. Would the constitutional safeguards in our present criminal justice system protect citizens from unwanted intrusions of this sort? Surprisingly, when one considers the current approach to the "reasonable expectation of privacy" pursuant to section 8 of the Charter, adopted by our courts in the context of other imaging technologies used in the war against drugs, it is uncertain whether we would be protected without clarification from our Supreme Court or the introduction of new legislation.

Several courts across Canada have already been called upon to determine whether heat patterns, electrical activities, or odours emanating from a private source carry a reasonable expectation of privacy once they enter public space (R. v. Kang Brown; R. v. A.M.; R. v. Tran; and R. v. Ly). In answering this question, a number of courts have interpreted the Supreme Court of Canada's decision in R. v. Tessling (2004) as standing for the proposition that, once bits of information emanate into a public space, they are no longer private and are therefore not subject to constitutional protection.

In this article we argue that this interpretation of R. v. Tessling is flawed and that, as brain scanning technologies increase in their ability to monitor and measure electrical information escaping from the skull, this mistake could have disastrous consequences for personal privacy. In the face of the R. v. Tessling decision, which intentionally conflated the distinctions between "bodily," "territorial," and "informational" privacy, we assert that the interception of brainwaves emanating from the skull, though functionally similar to the heat emanations at issue in R. v. Tessling, are not analogous. We briefly contemplate the implications in light of broader considerations of "brain privacy" in the future. In section 1 of this article, we discuss the Supreme Court's approach to privacy in R. v. Tessling (2004) and the manner in which that case has been subsequently applied in courts across Canada. Section 2 examines the current state of neuro-imaging technology and its potential application in the criminal justice system. In section 3, we investigate the potential application of R. v. Tessling to brain scans and the need to implicate other Charter rights, such as the right to security of the person (Charter, s. 7). In section 4, we discuss its future implications for brain privacy.

I. The R. v. Tessling analogy

In the Canadian criminal justice system, a central aspect of the right to privacy is contained within "the right to be secure against unreasonable search or seizure" (Charter of Rights and Freedoms, s. 8). In determining the scope of this right, courts generally ask whether the police interfered with a person's "reasonable expectation of privacy" (Bailey 2008). There have been many important section 8 cases, the most relevant in the current context is R. v. Tessling.

In R. v. Tessling (2004), the Supreme Court of Canada was asked to determine whether the Royal Canadian Mounted Police (RCMP) infringed upon the right to privacy when one of its planes flew over Mr Tessling's house one night without a warrant and fired infrared beams against its walls, measuring the escaping heat in order to determine whether he had a grow op in his basement. The Supreme Court decided that, because the escaping heat was freely available and easily measured in a public space without entering Mr Tessling's home, and because the heat patterns were, on their own, meaningless insofar as they did not reveal core biographical information about Mr Tessling, his "right to be secure against unreasonable search or seizure" remained intact. The Supreme Court concluded that these activities did not interfere with Mr Tessling's privacy, nor did they constitute a police search in a manner that ought to attract Charter scrutiny.

Writing for a unanimous Court, Justice Binnie overturned the decision of the Ontario Court of Appeal, where Justice Abella had decided in favour of Mr Tessling. Justice Abella focused on the broad intention of the police in using the infrared technology, which was to gain information about activities going on inside the home without a warrant. At the Supreme Court, Justice Binnie rejected this philosophical approach, choosing instead to focus on the actual capability of the infrared camera used by the RCMP. According to Justice Binnie, the RCMP's infrared picture taken that night was

> more accurately characterized as an external search for information about the home which may or may not be capable of giving rise to an inference about what was actually going on inside, depending on what other information is available. (R. v. Tessling 2004 at para.27)

While explicitly recognizing the potential for gaining insight into the home by aggregating the information, Justice Binnie concluded,

> External patterns of heat distribution on the external surfaces of a house is not information in which the respondent had a reasonable expectation of privacy. The heat distribution, as stated, offers no insight into his private life, and reveals nothing of his "biographical core of personal information." Its disclosure scarcely affects the "dignity, integrity and autonomy" of the person whose house is subject of the FLIR image (Plant 1993: p. 293). (R. v. Tessling 2004 at para. 63)

In addition, Justice Binnie was adamant that each technology should be addressed individually according to its present capacity:

> [T]echnology must be evaluated according to its present capability. Whatever evolution occurs in future will have to be dealt with by the courts step by step. Concerns should be addressed as they truly arise. (R. v. Tessling 2004 at para. 55; original emphasis)

Despite this clear call for a case-by-case approach, several courts across Canada have since been quick to generalize the R. v. Tessling decision by way of analogy, drawing a comparison between "external patterns of heat distribution on the external surfaces of a house" and other kinds of information that emanate from a private source into a public space (Kerr and McGill 2007).

The R. v. Tessling analogy has recently been adopted in the "sniffer dog" cases, where police dogs are used to detect the odour of drugs emanating from the private contents contained in a piece of luggage (R. v. Kang Brown 2006). For example, the Provincial Court for New Brunswick made a direct analogy between drug odours emanating from a duffle bag and heat emanations in R. v. Tessling, noting that the accused had knowingly exposed the odour to the public (R. v. McLay). In this case and in many other sniffer dog cases, the courts have relied on the R. v. Tessling analogy to conclude that individuals do not hold a reasonable expectation of privacy in external information emanations. The very same approach has been adopted with digital recording ammeters (DRA) used to detect emanations of electricity in and out of a home (R. v. Tran; R. v. Ly).

Crown attorneys in future emanation cases are sure to cite the R. v. Tessling analogy as a precedent for the following general rule, paraphrasing Justice Binnie:

> [E]xternal patterns of IX] on the external surfaces of [Y] is not information in which a respondent has a reasonable expectation of privacy. (R. v. Tessling 2004 at para. 63)

While the logic of this general analogy offers elegant explanatory surface appeal, its broad application would have serious negative consequences and in fact requires a significant intellectual leap. By reducing potentially coercive or restrictive state action to atoms, molecules, bits and bytes escaping from a building, backpack, or electrical device, by stripping police investigation entirely of its social context, this reductionist approach makes it practically irresistible to think of the information that is emanating into public space as "meaningless" insofar as it does not, by itself, reveal any core biographical information. The R. v. Tessling analogy therefore has the potential to substantially diminish the scope of section 8 protection in a manner that can only have the effect of significantly shrinking our reasonable expectations of privacy.

What are the implications of this analogy for technologies used to measure brainwaves emanating from our skulls? After describing the technologies that do so and their likely future use within the criminal justice system in section 2, we shall try to answer this question in section 3.

2. Brain scans and lie detection

Using high-powered magnets to intercept, monitor, and map brainwaves leaking from the skull as a means of determining the truth in a criminal trial would have sounded as bizarre to an attendee of the trials in Salem, 1692, as the notion of "trial by tire" sounds to us today. And yet, this could be where we are heading.

Two neuro-imaging techniques, in particular, have shown promise in brain-scan lie-detection: electro-encephalogram (EEG) and functional magnetic resonance imaging (fMRI) (Ford 2006).

An EEG measures the electrical activity within the brain via external sensors (Wolpe, Foster, and Langleban 2005). It is cost-effective and non-invasive. It measures electrical activity with great precision but lacks the sensitivity to determine exactly where in the brain this activity is occurring (Illes and Racine 2005; Wolpe et al. 2005). The EEG has been employed by researchers as a significantly improved version of the polygraph machine in a technique called "brain-fingerprinting" (Farwell and Smith 2001). The premise underlying this technique is that the brain releases a recognizable electric signal when processing a particular memory. Unlike the polygraph, which measures and records physiological factors, the EEG is used to measure the brain itself. Using this technique, a subject is shown a quick succession of relevant words and pictures, and the EEG measures the brainwaves spontaneously emitted by the brain in response. If the subject is shown something that is recognized, the brain will react by accessing the memory, and the EEG will, in turn, record that specific reaction.

The Iowa Supreme Court accepted brain-fingerprinting evidence in the case of Iowa v. Harrington. In that case, brain-fingerprinting was used to help exonerate a person wrongfully accused of murder 25 years after the conviction by demonstrating that he had no recognition of the crime scene.

Since that time, the scientist who performed the test on the accused, Lawrence Farwell, has patented the technique through a private company called Brain Fingerprinting Laboratories with the goal of commercializing it. Dr Farwell's claim is not that the technology establishes honesty. Rather, it determines whether specific information is or is not accessed by the brain. If a subject were shown a photo of a crime scene, the technique is said to establish whether there were preexisting memories of the crime scene (Farwell and Smith 2001). If the subject hears a specific sound, brain-fingerprinting determines whether the sound had been heard before. From a law-enforcement perspective, what is remarkable about this technology--assuming it could ever live up to its current hype--is its potential to enable significant transparency. Unless the technology can be circumvented, a suspect interrogated by question and answer would not be able to pick and choose which thoughts to keep private. Should it ever come to pass, a fully functioning version of the technology employed in police investigations or the courts could allow the state to, so to speak, "Google" critical facts within the brain of an accused, not exactly as a computer searches a hard drive but with a similar effect--determining whether the memory of a crime scene or murder weapon resides in the data banks of the accused's brain. At least, that is how the technology is sold. (2)

While EEG brain-fingerprinting may have the potential to uncover information that an accused person might wish to keep private, it does not directly detect deception. Functional magnetic resonance imaging, however, seeks to do just that. It is non-invasive and readily available, but the machinery is expensive and difficult to maintain (Illes and Racine 2005). It requires rather large machinery, though that may not continue to be the case in the coming decades. It functions by placing the subject's skull into a magnetic field and then bombarding it with radio waves (Kozel, Revell, Lorberbaum, Shastri, Elhai, Horner, Smith, Nahas, Bohning, and George 2004). The fMRI uses the different magnetic signatures of oxygenated and deoxygenated blood to measure blood flow within the brain. Active areas of the brain require more oxygenated blood than non-active areas. Traditionally, subjects lay on a table with their heads surrounded by a large cylindrical magnet like the familiar computed axial tomography (CAT) scan. Recently, however, designers have begun to create patient-friendly versions with less intimidating readers, raising the possibility in the coming decades of surreptitious use.

The usefulness of fMRI as an alternative approach to truth verification and lie detection is already being tested (Kozel et al. 2004; Langleben, Loughead, Bilker, Ruparel, Childress, Busch, and Gur 2005). Langleben et al. (2005) used fMRI technology to study the neural patterns associated with deception. Male volunteers were attached to an fMRI machine and were instructed to either truthfully or falsely confirm or deny having a particular playing card. When the participants gave truthful answers, the fMRI data showed increased activity in certain areas of the brain. When they provided deliberately deceptive answers, additional areas of their brain (parietal and frontal lobes) were activated. These data, along with the results of previous studies (Ganis, Kosslyn, Stose, Thompson, and Yurgelun-Todd 2003; Langleben, Schroeder, Maldjian, Gur, McDonald, Ragland, O'Brien, and Childress 2002; Lee, Liu, Tan, Chan, Mahankali, Feng, Hou, Fox, and Gao 2002) suggest that truth is the baseline condition and that deception is the inhibition of the truth. In other words, telling lies requires more neural circuits than telling the truth. Whenever a person attempts to deceive, additional oxygenated blood is required. One advantage of fMRI is its ability to map the relevant brain regions involved in deception, a process that cannot be achieved by EEG brain-fingerprinting. The potential of fMRI in lie detection is significant. The brain acts differently when inventing rather than remembering information--and fMRI can detect that difference (Lee et al. 2002).

EEG and fMRI have both enjoyed much positive attention in the scientific community and in the popular press (Abbott 2001; Talbot 2007). While neither technique has been broadly adopted in the criminal justice system yet, it is not difficult to imagine that technological advances could provide sufficient reliability to gain widespread acceptance in the near future. As noted above, one U.S. court has already accepted EEG brain-fingerprinting as evidence in Iowa v. Harrington. Canadian courts will no doubt have to grapple with similar issues. Whether these technologies will ever measure up to Wonder Woman's "Lasso of Truth" as a means of inducing truth-telling is speculative at best (Moulton 1943). There is certainly no shortage of hype in the literature (Talbot 2007).

3. Tessling on my brain

When considering the future of brain scanning in the criminal justice system, it is interesting to contemplate how courts might approach the emerging issue of brain privacy. Given the preceding discussion, it is obvious that brain scanning could have an enormous impact on Charter rights: not only on the reasonable expectation of privacy that accompanies the right to be secure against unreasonable search and seizure (Charter: s. 8) but also on the right against self-incrimination (Charter: s. 11c) and the right to security of the person (Charter: s. 7). While these are subjects of our ongoing research, the focus of our discussion in this section is the reasonable expectation of privacy standard discussed above in section 1.

R. v. Tessling remains the leading case on the reasonable expectation of privacy and the case most on point for a discussion of surreptitious brain scanning. Recall that the Supreme Court said in that case,

> External patterns of heat distribution on the external surfaces of a house is not information in which the respondent had a reasonable expectation of privacy.

According to the Court, heat information available on the outside of Mr Tessling's house was not protected because the information was, on its own, meaningless, because the heat patterns themselves did not reveal core biographical information about Mr Tessling.

The same analysis might be said to apply if the technology in question was not an infrared scan of Mr Tessling's house but a remote scanning of his brain. Brain-scanning technologies measure external patterns of electricity (and magnetism) on the external surfaces of the skull-information that is, on its own, "meaningless." If neuro-imaging technologies really could scan the brain the way a computer scans a hard drive, then there would be a strong argument to support the claim that brain scans are not meaningless, since they would clearly reveal intimate details about an individual's life. However, this is not the current state of the art. EEG scans determine merely whether information is recognized by the subject, and fMRI scans can only pinpoint brain activity; neither can actually read a person's mind in a way that WIRED magazine and other popular culture sources would have us believe (Silberman 2006; Talbot 2007). These technologies, at best, provide indications of knowledge and honesty. In essence, this is analogous to the heat patterns in R. v. Tessling, which merely indicated activities occurring in his house (because thermal imaging cannot differentiate heat produced by a sauna or fireplace from heat produced by a grow op). Because brain scans, on their own, cannot differentiate or determine thoughts in any meaningful way, one might argue that the scan itself is likewise not a search and that the R. v. Tessling analogy applies: external patterns of electricity on the external surfaces of a skull is not information in which a person has a reasonable expectation of privacy.

Although, on its face, the R. v. Tessling analogy appears solid, there are differences in the nature and quality of the information collected by neuro-imaging technologies that have the potential to undermine the analogy. These differences revolve around the "personal" nature of the brain information.

In her more detailed discussion of R. v. Tessling earlier in this special issue, Professor Jane Bailey outlines three tiers of privacy protection recognized by Canadian courts: (i) personal, (ii) territorial, and (iii) informational. As she points out, personal privacy enjoys the highest level of protection, informational the lowest. As Justice Binnie put it,

> Privacy of the person perhaps has the strongest claim to constitutional shelter because it protects bodily integrity, and in particular the right not to have our bodies touched or explored to disclose objects or matters we wish to conceal. (R. v. Tessling 2004 at para. 21)

Professor Bailey rightly asserts that the Supreme Court's decision to characterize heat emanations from Mr Tessling's home as implicating "informational privacy" (rather than, say, "territorial privacy") affected the outcome by placing it into a less protected category (Bailey 2008: 302). If the heat patterns had been deemed "territorial" (or, better yet, "personal"), they would have enjoyed a higher level of privacy protection. Do patterns of electricity emanating from the brain likewise implicate "informational privacy" interests, or are they of a more "personal" nature? How ought courts to deal with this intersectionality when essentially every bit of surveillance evidence can be reduced to raw information?

Applying the Tessling analogy, the electrical activities collected during a brain scan can be characterized as information about the brain rather than a search of the brain, in which case they would, like Tessling, fall into the category of informational rather than personal privacy.

Without question, the manner in which the courts will characterize brain emanations in the future will have a significant impact on the ultimate outcome. To illustrate, recall that the Ontario Court of Appeal decision in R. v. Tessling (2003) characterized police use of thermal imaging as implicating territorial privacy (the second-highest level of privacy protection), thereby concluding that the infrared picture constituted an unreasonable search. By contrast, the Supreme Court characterized police use of thermal imaging as implicating informational privacy (the lowest level of privacy protection), thereby concluding that police use of FLIR did not constitute an unreasonable search. Only if brain information is considered "personal" will it enjoy a higher level of privacy protection than Mr Tessling's heat emanations. But does the information collected by brain scans meet this standard for protection?

The basis of a standard was established by the Supreme Court in R. v. Plant. Like R. v. Tessling, the facts of the case involved police reacting to informant tips about marijuana grow ops. In R. v. Plant, the police accessed the computer records of Plant's hydro provider and discovered abnormally high electrical usage, leading to a closer inspection of his home, a search warrant, and ultimately an arrest. Justice Sopinka decided that the hydro records were not private information:

> [I]n order for constitutional protection to be extended, the information seized must be of a "personal and confidential" nature. In fostering the underlying values of dignity, integrity and autonomy, it is fitting that s. 8 of the Charter should seek to protect a biographical core of personal information which individuals in a free and democratic society would wish to maintain and control from dissemination to the state. This would include information which tends to reveal intimate details of the lifestyle and personal choices of the individual. (R. v. Plant at 293)

Canadian courts have not yet clearly articulated what constitutes a "biographical core of personal information" other than by enumeration. For example, according to the Supreme Court in Plant, information gathered from hydro records is not. According to the Alberta Court of Appeal, odour emanations from a backpack are not (R. v. Kang Brown). Personal information like name (R. v. Harris) and DNA (R. v. Peddle) may be or may not be, depending on the context. Breath samples (R. v. Padavattan) and items placed in the garbage do not qualify (R. v. Patrick) but a personal diary definitely qualifies (R. v. Shearing).

Two additional Supreme Court decisions are useful in the determination of whether the information obtained using brain scans is "personal."

In R v. Dyment, the court made it clear that personal privacy is paramount, indicating that it is often implicated in the use of a person's body:

> [T]he use of a person's body without his consent
> to obtain information about him, invades an area
> of personal privacy essential to the maintenance
> of his human dignity. (para. 27)

A surreptitious brain scan would allow the police to gather information about a person from his or her body without that person's consent or control. However, the information gathering does not directly affect a person's body. Brain scans fall somewhere between the removal of bodily samples (like blood or hair) and the measuring of heat patterns emanating from Mr Tessling's home. Brain waves are involuntarily emitted from the brain but do not represent tangible matter in any sense that constitutes the physical person. While brain emanations into public space do not fit easily into the category of bodily specimens and samples, they certainly do involve and implicate the body. On this basis, brain scans could be understood as "personal" rather than merely "informational," thus weakening the R. v. Tessling analogy. If evidence gathered by brain scans is understood as bodily information then, according to R. v. Dyment, its non-consensual use does violate personal privacy.

The second additional Supreme Court privacy decision worthy of consideration is Dagg v. Canada. In that case, relying on Alan Westin's seminal work (Westin 1967), the court held that

> privacy is grounded in physical and moral
> autonomy--the freedom to engage in one's own
> thoughts, actions, decisions.(para. 65)

Whereas thermal imaging can detect only the presence of heat (coinciding with heat-generating activities going on in the house), neuro-imaging has the potential to gather information about the brain (coinciding with the thoughts and memories of an individual). Effective neuro-imaging technologies would not read minds but, if used surreptitiously or beyond the scope of an individual's consent, they could one day interfere with an individual's autonomy by removing the ability of the individual to control the knowledge or dissemination of important personal information about himself or herself. If brain scans are ever actually able to drastically reduce or remove the potential for deceit, they would undermine moral autonomy. As the Kantian dictum goes, "Ought implies can" (Kant 1997: chap. 8) If one cannot do otherwise, one is no longer acting within the realm of morality. Morality entails the ability to choose. When one is compelled to tell the truth--whether by Wonder Woman's lasso of truth, by torture, or with a No Lie fMRI[TM] device (3)--that person is precluded from the possibility of full moral agency. Aside from being unable to morally praise that person for telling the truth, how could we say that this person is a moral actor if she can no longer freely engage in her own thoughts and decisions?

4. The Future of Brain Privacy

The fact that the neuroscience community is aggressively pursuing lie-detection techniques, combined with the fact that the criminal justice system is interested in employing reliable versions of these technologies, suggests that brain privacy is likely to emerge as a significant legal issue. However, it is unlikely to emerge in the context of reasonable expectations of privacy, as discussed above. That context presumes the far-off possibility of surreptitious and remote brain scanning. Still, in our view, there is value in such speculation.

Whether the technology arrives or not, Tessling-on-my-brain sheds light on the shortcomings of the current approach to information emanation in a number of ways. First, it provides a reductio ad absurdum in response to the hypothesis that a general privacy rule should govern all information emanations. There are good reasons to treat heat patterns, drug odours, brain waves, and other forms of emanation differently in different contexts. The R. v. Tessling decision was never meant to provide a single rule. Second, the example also illustrates an important distinction between predictive and normative expectations--while it may be reasonable to predict that information will emanate from private to public spaces and that new technologies will be able to measure and monitor those emanations, it does not follow that we cannot reasonably expect to maintain privacy in at least some of that information. As Justice Binnie said, "Expectation of privacy is a normative rather than a descriptive standard" (R. v. Tessling 2004). Third, the example highlights problems with the current trifurcated privacy hierarchy (personal/territorial/informational). In a world where so many things can be reduced to bits and bytes of information, a privacy hierarchy that gives very little weight to information and no reliable means of determining which privacy category applies risks too much. Is a brain wave merely information or should we consider it part of a person? How do we deal with an intersectionality of privacy interests where more than one zone of privacy is implicated? Neither scholars nor our courts have addressed any of these questions. The Tessling-on-my-brain example illustrates the need for a more robust theory of privacy.

Although there is much to learn about brain privacy from these speculations, the three issues most likely to arise in the near future pertain to (i) the nature of consent, (ii) the right against self-incrimination, and (iii) security of the person.

The consent issues are not new ones. There are at least two aspects. The first relates to the tort law concept of consent to treatment (Solomon, Kostal, and McInnes 2003: 161). If a lie-detection procedure involves any risk of harm to the body, a failure to obtain consent could result in an action for battery (Downie, Caulfield, and Flood 2007: 90). But what if there are no negative health implications? There is still a consent issue in the context of informational privacy. The challenge here is also not a novelty. Even assuming a voluntary and informed consent, the problem of secondary uses of the information is sure to arise (Personal Information Protection and Electronic Documents Act 4.5 Principle 5). How do we ensure that brain scans undertaken for one purpose are not collected, used, or disclosed for some other purpose? Although these issues are not new ones, they will have new currency in a world where employers, insurance companies, bankers, teachers, lovers, lawyers, law-enforcement agencies, and judges all clamour to learn more about a person's brain states.

The second issue likely to emerge is the risk against self-incrimination; the Charter protects individuals against being forced to act as a witness against themselves (Charter: ss. 11c, 13). The state is required to prove all aspects of a crime without the assistance of the accused. Neuro-imaging techniques have the potential to remove individuals from their role as the gatekeeper of their own personal information, bypassing them by simply seizing the information from snapshots of their brain activity. Dr Farwell's claim that brain-fingerprinting can determine if an individual recognizes a particular person, place, or thing could be used to exonerate, but could just as easily be used to violate Charter protections against self-incrimination. Future courts are sure to be called upon to determine whether the information gained via brain scans is protected as a result of its potential for self-incrimination or whether it is not protected, like breathalyzer information, because the protection applies only to statements (R. v. Stasiuk).

The third issue likely to emerge reflects the fact that neuro-imaging has clear potential to intrude on the physical and psychological autonomy of the individual. Tessling-on-my-brain presents the moral intuition that brain emanations are somehow fundamentally different from emanations of heat from a house, odour from a suitcase, etc. Section 7 of the Charter clarifies that intuition. It protects the life, liberty, and security of the person of all Canadians (Charter: s. 7). The Supreme Court has determined that security of the person protects both the physical and psychological integrity of the individual (R. v. Rodriguez at para. 21). For example, security of the person has been applied to protect against psychological stress caused by removing children from the care of their parents (New Brunswick (Min. Health & Community Services) v. G. (J.)). It is unclear whether section 7 would be found to protect against brain scans, but the issue will likely arise in the context of brain-scan lie detection. In a society that is ordered around risk (Beck 1992; Giddens 1999) and sees technology as the antidote, the connection between privacy and security is apparent.

5. Conclusion

It is difficult to draw a tidy conclusion with clear policy recommendations about a technology still in the laboratory. This article is meant more as an appreciation of what lurks around the corner. As the art and science of discovering and understanding the information that emanates from our brains surges toward the future, proliferating exponentially in an era where our intelligence will become increasingly non-biological and trillions of rimes more powerful than it is today (Kurzweil 2005), we suggest that the goal of using brain-based lie detecrion in our criminal justice system will require better-developed theories of privacy.

If we are to maintain our "dignity, integrity and autonomy" (R. v. Plant) in the face of emerging brain-surveillance techniques that might one day be capable of retelling the stories of our personal lives with or without our permission and yet in ways that are personally and territorially unobtrusive, scholars and jurists must confront the social implications of informational privacy much more deeply than they have, interrogating its normative implications in an empirical universe of information emanation.

References & Cases Law Omitted

Ian Kerr
Faculty of Law, Faculty of Medicine, Department of Philosophy, University of Ottawa
Max Binnie and Cynthia Aoki
Faculty of Law, University of Ottawa

Notes

(1.) The authors wish to express their thanks to the Social Sciences and Humanities Research Council, the Canada Research Chairs Program, Bell Canada, and the Ontario Research Network in Electronic Commerce for their generous contributions to the funding of the research project from which this article is derived. Thanks also to Professor Jane Bailey and Professor Valerie Steeves for their insightful feedback, which substantially improved the quality of this article.

(2.) See http://www.brainwavescience.com.

(3.) See http://www.noliemri.com/index.htm.

23

Surfing Brain Waves: fMRI* for Lie Detection

A Possible New Lie-Detector Technology

M. E. Kabay

O ne of the critical steps in incident response is the interview. In previous articles in this column ("Poly want a hacker?" "Drawing the Lines" and "Blurred Lines") I've looked briefly at the use of polygraph as a tool for identifying lies. Today, I will look at another technology for telling truth from fiction: functional magnetic resonance imaging (fMRI).

I have a personal interest in fMRI because my wife, Dr D. N. Black, MDCM, FRCP(C), a neuropsychologist for 25 years, has turned me into what we describe as "that most useless of hobbyists, an amateur neurologist." She often describes patient symptoms and asks me to come up with a diagnosis - a bizarre but enjoyable version of 20 questions. Sometimes I'm even right. I've actually had the privilege of serving as her statistician in some of her papers, but my favorite is our 1987 letter in the Canadian Medical Association Journal about a new sleep disorder.

*fMRI: functional magnetic resonance imaging

Source: Surfing brain waves; MRI for lie detection; A possible new lie-detector technology. Network World, January 8, 2009.

128

fMRI is yet another development in the evolving study of brain function. Martha J. Farah and Paul Root Wolpe have an excellent overview of these technologies in their article, "Monitoring and Manipulating Brain Function: New Neuroscience Technologies and Their Ethical Implications" from the Hastings Center Report (May-June 2004) pp 35-45. Using strong external magnetic fields, fMRI systems measure blood flow - and thus the level of neuronal activity - with a resolution of a millimeter or less and a response time of about 1 second.

One interesting application of fMRI has been to identify patterns of brain activity associated with truthful statements compared with lies, as Kozel et al. reported in 2004 (Journal of Neuropsychiatry and Clinical Neuroscience 16(3):295-305). Early results were inconclusive: "Specific brain regions were activated during deception, but the present technique lacks good predictive power for individuals."

Reporting on later research by Faro et al., reporter Beth W. Orenstein wrote in an article entitled, "Guilty? Investigating fMRI's Future as a Lie Detector" (Radiology Today 6(10):30) that "The fMRI study found that when the subjects were telling lies, more areas of their brains activated than when they were being truthful." She quoted Dr Scott Faro, MD, professor and vice chair of Radiology at Philadelphia's famous Temple University School of Medicine: "Indeed, what we found was that approximately twice as many areas of the brain - 14 vs. seven - are activated when one is lying as compared to when one is telling the truth."

In Steve Silberman's 2006 article in Wired Magazine, "Don't Even Think About Lying", the author describes his experiences being scanned and discusses some of the growing controversy about the ethical implications of equipment that scans brain activity in the service of the state:

"So what began as a neurological inquiry into why kids with ADHD blurt out embarrassing truths may end up forcing the legal system to define more clearly the inviolable boundaries of the self."

"My concern is precisely with the civil and commercial uses of fMRI lie detection," says ethicist Wolpe. "When this technology is available on the market, it will be in places like Guantanamo Bay and Abu Ghraib in a heartbeat.

"Once people begin to think that police can look right into their brains and tell whether they're lying," he adds, "it's going to be 1984 in their minds, and there could be a significant backlash. The goal of detecting deception requires far more public scrutiny than it has had up until now. As a society, we need to have a very serious conversation about this."

At a symposium entitled "Will brain imaging be lie detector test of the future?" held at Harvard University in February 2007, several participants expressed skepticism about fMRI's applicability and reliability. For example, critics pointed out that some of the studies of reliability failed to use realistic scenarios involving stressful situations; they also ignored well-established "countermeasures for defeating the fMRI, like performing mental arithmetic - or simply fidgeting."

No Lie MRI, Inc. offers fMRI lie-detection services; its overview pages offer a number of interesting details, including this list of restrictions on the Process Overview page:

> Currently the only known limitations to the technology developed by No Lie MRI are:
> - Individuals can not have metal inside their body
> - Individuals can not be claustrophobic
> - Individuals can not be brain damaged
> - Individuals can not move around during the MRI scanning process

No Lie MRI provides a video showing a simulated test.

CEPHOS Corp. also offers fMRI services. In its discussion of the legal admissibility of the new technology, the company predicts that "Cephos fMRI lie detection evidence are [sic] likely admissible in court" and provides a number of arguments on why the technology is likely to pass the Daubert Test on admissibility of expert testimony on scientific evidence.

Security practitioners will want to continue monitoring (no pun intended) developments in fMRI to see if the technology can provide useful, reliable indications of truthfulness and deception in our investigations.

24

Professor Dubious about New Lie Detectors

A
U.S. professor says she is unconvinced new technologies such as functional magnetic resonance imaging are superior to polygraph tests for detecting lies.

University of Illinois Professor Melissa Littlefield says in today's forensically sophisticated, "CSI"-influenced world, polygraphy -- which bases its results on functions of the autonomic nervous system -- is being increasingly dismissed as dated and unreliable.

"Functional magnetic resonance imaging and Brain Fingerprinting have been hailed as the next, best technologies for lie detection C*," Littlefield said. "Far from describing the brain and its functions, fMRI and Brain Fingerprinting produce models of the brain that reinforce social notions of deception, truth and deviance."

Littlefield said she's unconvinced the new technologies are necessarily superior to the old ones and she advises caution when considering the promise of brain-based truth-seeking technologies.

"This 9/11 kind of hype has allowed and fueled this desire both in scientists and the media, and in popular culture, to try to find something to hold onto for security's sake," she said. "But I don't think it's really there" -- at least not yet."

Her research appears in the May issue of the journal Science, Technology & Human Values.

Source: Professor dubious about new lie detectors. UPI NewsTrack, June 2, 2009.

25

True Lies: Cutting-Edge Technology Has Renewed the Search for a Better Lie Detector

Some Show Promise, But They Have Yet to be Tested in Court

Mark Hansen

I AM A TERRORIST.

At least that's what I've been told to be, as I'm sitting at a computer in the lab adjacent to J. Peter Rosenfeld's cluttered second-floor office in the psychology department on Northwestern University's leafy campus.

Electrodes are attached to my scalp, behind each ear, above and below my left eye, and in the middle of my forehead.

I'm thinking about how I can lay waste to the city of Houston. Or rather, trying not to think about it. After all, I am a terrorist; and I'm

---

Source: True Lies: cutting-edge technology has renewed the search for a better lie detector. Some show promise, but they have yet to be tested in court. ABA Journal, October 2009, v95 i10 p56(7).

trying to conceal the fact that I want to lay waste to the nation's fourth-largest city.

Rosenfeld, who for 20 years has been studying brain wave activity as a means of detecting deception, has been describing a new test protocol he has designed to catch terrorists before they can execute a planned attack. And when he offered me a chance to be tested, I said, "Hook me up."

The premise of the test is that a suspect who knows details of the plan--the location, the method and the timing--will emit a telltale response from brain waves when presented with information that coincides with those details, no matter how hard the suspect tries to conceal it.

"If you had a suspected terrorist in custody and you had some idea what he was planning to do next, you could give him this test," says Rosenfeld, a pioneer in the field of neuroscience-based lie detection. "You wouldn't have to waterboard him, and you'd extract better information out of him, too."

Before strapping up, I had been given a packet of instructions and a briefing for a mock terrorist attack--a list of U.S. cities, months and weapons--and told to circle any of the items that have a special meaning, such as a place I've lived, the month I was born or any weaponry I am particularly fond of or familiar with.

I was informed that my "commander" has chosen to attack Houston with a bomb in July, but I'm supposed to recommend one of four specific Houston locations--airport, downtown, etc.--for the attack. I'm given the pros and cons; and when I've made my decision, I'm told to e-mail the commander with my recommendation and the reasoning behind it. I've done all that, and my plot is good to go.

Once wired, I am seated before a computer monitor with a five-button control box in my left hand and a two-button control box in my right. As the test begins, the names of half a dozen cities appear momentarily on the screen, followed by a single line of six identical numbers.

Each time a city appears, I'm to press randomly one of the buttons in my left hand, trying not to follow any particular pattern or repetition. When a sequence of numbers appears, I'm to press "yes" if the numbers "111111" appear and "no" for any other numbers.

The electrodes on my scalp measure brain waves, I'm told. The ones around my eye measure eye movements, which can create artifacts in the brain waves. The ones behind the ears control for electrical "noise" in the room or the amplifiers. The one on my forehead is a ground.

While we take a few minutes to practice, the whole experience seems to me surprisingly unsophisticated. The computer looks like something out of the 1980s; the "lab" like somebody's dorm room. The research assistants look more like college kids than scientists. Where's all the splashy, colorful, three-dimensional, computer-generated imagery? What's up with the buttons?

Then the real test begins.

A city flashes. Then another, followed by several more cities in quick succession. Then a string of numbers. More cities, more numbers. I'm pressing buttons as fast as my fingers will move, trying not to blink or press the same button twice while keeping track of which city I've just seen. (The examiner occasionally asks, just to make sure that I'm paying attention.)

At first I do OK. But monotony and fatigue set in. I realize I've pushed the same button two or three times in a row. Then I catch myself pushing a button with my left hand when I'm supposed to be using my right. I'm starting to blink every time I push a button.

Some 300 city-number combinations later, it's over. It's only one part of a three-part test, but my fingers hurt. My mind is mush. My eyes burn from trying to keep them open the entire time.

The buttons and numbers are designed to keep me from specifically thinking about Houston, my putative target. The process is designed to replicate diversion techniques that a skilled terrorist might use to shield against a lie detector.

But when the examiner shows me a screen shot of my test results, I know I'd make a lousy terrorist: My brain waves have registered a huge dip downward--a positive response--each time the word Houston appeared on the screen.

It turns out my results are consistent with other, more formal tests by Rosenfeld and his team. Analyzing the data from one recent study, they were able to confirm through brain waves the "guilt" of all 12 subjects identified as "terrorists" in the mock exercise, without incorrectly identifying any "innocent" subjects as guilty. Even analyzing subjects on a blind basis, they were able to correctly identify 10 out of 12 guilty subjects without misidentifying any innocents. Moreover, in their analysis of the guilty, they were also able to correctly identify two-thirds of the details of the planned, hypothetical attack.

NEW TOOLS, NEW URGENCY

While the development of an effective lie detector has been a goal since ancient times, research into deception detection had been all but dormant for decades.

But the 9/11 terrorist attacks and the ensuing debate over the use of torture and other questionable means of collecting and corroborating information have given new urgency to the search for a better lie detector. And many of the most promising--and controversial--lines of inquiry are linked to recent advances in neuroscience and new applications of long-standing bio-measurement devices and techniques.

Rosenfeld's truth detection experiment, for instance, relies on the use of electroencephalography, which monitors electrical signals to localize and quantify brain activity. The EEG is commonly used to help diagnose epilepsy, Alzheimer's disease and other neurological disorders, as well as some mental illnesses, like schizophrenia.

There is also a growing fascination with the possibilities of magnetic resonance imaging and positron emission tomography scans to reveal otherwise hidden evidence of deception or guilt.

Yet these new truth technologies have yet to be tested in court. Overconfident marketing, conflicting scientific claims and worries about overdependence on technology have made some wary of the effect on justice.

"Because the MRI is a big, fancy machine that produces these beautiful color pictures, there's a fear that people might be overly impressed by the technology and take it more seriously than they should," says Hank Greely, a professor of law and genetics at Stanford University who also heads the law school's Center for Law and the Biosciences.

"On the other hand, because the EEG only produces an image of a brain wave, people may not give it the attention it deserves, even though at this point, we don't know which technique, if either, will ever be effective at lie detection."

That's been the problem with lie detection for decades. The most recognized tool we have is the polygraph, which has been around for nearly 100 years. But the polygraph doesn't even measure deception per se. It measures physiological features associated with stress or anxiety, such as systolic blood pressure, heart rate, breathing rate and galvanic skin response.

And it isn't considered particularly reliable in scientific circles. The polygraph has an accuracy rate of about 70 to 90 percent, depending on the examiner. And it can be beaten by sociopaths and people who are good at suppressing their emotions.

Gary Ridgway, the so-called Green River Killer, passed a polygraph early on in his killing spree and went on to kill 48 women. And CIA double agent Aldrich Ames passed two polygraph exams during the nine years he spent as a Russian spy.

DECEPTION AND DETECTION

The next empirical attempt to develop an effective lie detector was through voice stress analysis, the origins of which date back to the 1940s. Voice stress analysis purports to measure physiological changes in the muscles of the voice box that are thought to be associated with deception.

But voice stress analysis suffers from the same basic defect as the polygraph: It attempts to measure deception indirectly, through the stress purportedly associated with telling a lie. And while proponents claim high levels of accuracy, empirical tests have been far from encouraging. One study showed close to chance levels of success in identifying deception in mock crime situations. Another study deemed it unsuccessful in detecting spontaneous lies in a simulated job interview.

"The scientific research on it has been universally negative," Greely says.

Though voice stress analysis is apparently quite popular among law enforcement agencies, that seems to have more to do with the fact that it is relatively inexpensive and can be quite intimidating than with its ability to detect lying, experts say.

"It's pretty good at telling whether somebody is nervous or not, but a lot of people get nervous when they're talking to the police," Greely says.

The search for an EEG-based lie detector got its start in the 1980s, when researchers first identified one particular type of brain wave, known as the P300, that appears particularly useful in detecting deception.

[Graphic omitted]

According to the researchers, involuntary, split-second bumps in the P300, which occur about 300 milliseconds after a subject is exposed to a particular stimulus, are believed to indicate that the subject's brain "recognizes" the stimulus.

Proponents say the technique can be used to confirm or refute a subject's claims that he has or doesn't have information about a particular place or event or item--such as a crime scene or a planned terrorist attack or a murder weapon--stored in his brain, even if the subject is trying to hide it.

Rosenfeld is the first to admit that the technique has practical limitations. In the case of terrorism, it won't work if you have no clue what sort of concealed information you're looking for. In its application to everyday crime, a guilty suspect might be too drunk or high on drugs to remember the details of the crime he committed. And if such details are well-known among the general public, even an innocent subject would have "guilty" knowledge stored in his brain.

He also concedes that the technique is not yet ready for the courtroom. It still needs to be field-tested in the real world. And it must be shown to be effective against the use of countermeasures to evade detection, such as tapping a finger on the leg or repeating one's name to oneself over and over.

But Rosenfeld says the EEG-based approach has several practical advantages over other types of lie detection technology now being studied. It is relatively small, inexpensive and portable. It is also the only one being tested under simulated real-world conditions, like the mock terrorism scenario. And it is already proving in early trials to be highly resistant to the use of countermeasures.

"In general, about one out of 20 subjects will beat the test using countermeasures. But chances are we're going to catch them anyway because their reaction times will give them away," he says.

RECOGNITION AND MEMORY

Experts agree that the p300 wave is a well-established scientific phenomenon, and that the timing and shape of the P300 wave has meaning. But what that means at this point isn't exactly clear.

The fact that somebody "recognizes" something doesn't necessarily mean he's guilty of anything, they point out.

"Just because you recognize Osama bin Laden doesn't mean you spent time in an al-Qaida training camp with him," Greely says. "Maybe you just saw his picture on TV or the cover of a magazine."

By the same token, he adds, a suspect might recognize a crime scene because he committed the crime in question or because the crime took place at a Starbucks, the inside of which all tend to look alike.

The EEG-based approach also appears to misunderstand the nature of memory, which does not record and recall information like a videotape recorder but changes and adapts over time, other experts caution.

"Every time a memory is recalled, it is altered," says University of Akron law professor Jane Moriarty, an expert on scientific evidence.

Experts also say the credibility of this line of research has been undercut somewhat by the hype given to it by Lawrence Farwell, one of its leading proponents.

Farwell is a neuroscientist who left academia in the mid-1990s to launch Brain Fingerprinting Laboratories, which developed an EEG-based technique that purports to show whether an individual has specific information stored in his brain.

On its website, the company claims an extremely high accuracy rate for its patented technique, which Farwell puts at about 97 percent. In more than 200 tests, he says, the process has been correct all but six times. In those six cases, the results were indeterminate.

CLAIMS IN QUESTION

But Farwell's claims are widely discounted in the relevant scientific community. Critics say that there is little research--other than his own-- to back up his claims, and that he refuses to share his underlying data with others, asserting that his technique is proprietary.

[Graphic omitted] Nor is Farwell's credibility enhanced, critics say, by his inflated claims of judicial acceptance of the technique.

On his website, Farwell suggests that the Iowa Supreme Court overturned a murder conviction based in part on the results of a brain fingerprinting test on the defendant. But the court actually reversed the conviction for reasons unrelated to the brain fingerprinting evidence.

Rosenfeld has written an in-depth critique of Farwell's methodology and claims, which he concludes are "exaggerated and sometimes misleading." However, he ends his critique with a plea not to throw the proverbial baby out with the bathwater.

"Just because one person is attempting to commercialize brain-based deception-detection methods prior to completion of needed peer-reviewed research (with independent replication) does not imply that the several serious scientists who are now seriously pursuing this line of investigation should abandon their efforts," he writes.

But Farwell says he has gotten a bum rap from critics. Anyone who closely reviews the scientific literature will conclude that the fundamental science on which the technique is based is solid and well-established, he maintains. He also says he has disclosed his methodology, both to colleagues who have used it in their own studies and to the U.S. Patent Office in exchange for the four patents he has gotten on the technique. And he insists that brain fingerprinting "played a role" in the reversal of a defendant's murder conviction, albeit an indirect one.

"The important thing is that the brain fingerprinting evidence was admitted and that we got the right answer," he says. "That was no accident."

If Farwell's claims haven't given EEG-based lie detection research a bad name, the brain electrical oscillations signature test, which purports to build on his and other neuroscientists' work, might.

The BEOS test, invented by an Indian neuroscientist, purportedly can tell not only whether a subject recognizes the details of a crime, but whether the subject recognizes those details because of experiencing them or for some other reason.

The test, which police in two Indian states are using, has already led to the conviction of a married couple in the arsenic poisoning murder of the wife's former fiance. However, both defendants have since been released on bail while an appeals court reviews their convictions on grounds apparently unrelated to the BEOS evidence.

But critics are highly dubious. Greely says all anyone has seen of the technique is the inventor's own brochure. "I've yet to meet anybody who has any idea how what they claim to be doing would be possible," he says.

Rosenfeld says the technology has neither been peer-reviewed nor independently replicated. "As far as I'm concerned, it's not worth a dime."

One of the more promising of the new lie detection technologies on the horizon is fMRI, or functional magnetic resonance imaging. This is not just because it is the most studied of the techniques under development but because it is already being offered to the public by two private companies: No Lie MRI, which is based in San Diego, and the Cephos Corp., which is based in Tyngsboro, Mass.

In fact, an fMRI-based lie detection test came close to being offered into evidence for the first time in a U.S. court earlier this year. But the proffered evidence was voluntarily withdrawn at the last minute under mounting opposition from the scientific community.

The case was a juvenile protection hearing in San Diego involving a custodial parent accused of sex abuse. The defense was seeking to introduce a brain scan performed by No Lie MRI to prove the defendant was telling the truth when he denied sexually abusing the child.

The case file is sealed. San Diego lawyer Michael McGlinn, who represented the accused parent, refused to discuss the matter. But Joel Huizenga, the founder and CEO of No Lie MRI, says the decision not to use the evidence had nothing to do with the validity of the test, which he contends clearly showed the accused parent was being truthful.

Functional magnetic resonance imaging, which got its start in medical research in the early 1990s, allows scientists to create highly localized maps of the brain's networks in action as it processes thoughts, sensations, feelings, memories and motor commands. It basically works by tracking oxygenated blood flow to different parts of the brain in response to specific tasks, behaviors and affective states.

When the technology was first developed, it was used primarily as a diagnostic tool for disease and other neurological disorders. But researchers soon turned their attention to other possible uses, including detecting pain, predicting future behavior and studying the neurophysiological correlates of deception. The theory behind the use of fMRIs for lie detection is that lying requires the brain to do more work than telling the truth does.

Huizenga of No Lie MRI and his counterpart at Cephos, founder and CEO Steven Laken, say the technology is ready for the courtroom. Laken says there have been more than 12,000 peer-reviewed, published papers on fMRI technology itself, including nearly two dozen on its lie detection capabilities.

Laken also notes that the U.S. Supreme Court relied on fMRI-based evidence in 2005 when it outlawed the execution of juvenile offenders in Roper v. Simmons. And he says many judges have told him they believe it meets the admissibility standards for scientific evidence.

Huizenga suggests that fMRI testing, while not perfect, is far more accurate than other types of evidence that are routinely admitted in court, like eyewitness identifications and police lineups. "This is the first time in human history we've had anything that can tell scientifically and accurately whether somebody is lying," he says.

142

Few experts would dispute fMRI's potential value as a lie detector. But the vast majority of them seem to agree that it has a long way to go before it is proven reliable enough to be used in court. While they acknowledge that fMRI has produced some favorable results as a lie detector in the laboratory setting, they say the research to date suffers from several flaws.

STILL IN THE DISCOVERY PHASE

All of the studies involved relatively small samples. The majority have not tried to assess deception on an individual level. Only a handful of the results have been replicated by others. And most of the experiments have been done on healthy young adults. No one has tested children, the elderly or people with physical or mental illnesses.

Researchers, moreover, have often disagreed on what regions of the brain are associated with deception. Most of the experiments have involved low-stakes tasks, such as picking a playing card or remembering a three-digit number. And only a few have tried to assess the effectiveness of the technique when subjects employ countermeasures.

Moriarty says the studies raise as many questions as they answer.

"For now, the most that can be said is that the preliminary data are fascinating but sparse," she says. "While there is little doubt that fMRI--as a machine--works well, there are innumerable questions about the extent of what can be stated with certainty about the interpretation of the images generated."

Greely, who co-authored a 2007 study that found "very little" in the peer-reviewed literature to suggest that fMRI-based lie detection might be useful in real-word situations, says he hasn't seen anything since then that would change his mind.

"At this point, we just don't know how well these methods will work with diverse subjects in real-world situations, with or without the use of countermeasures," he says.

Also, fMRI-based lie detectors would present practical limitations. The scanners are big, bulky and expensive to own and operate. Test subjects can't be claustrophobic or have any metal in their bodies. They also must be cooperative and compliant in order to be tested, leaving some experts skeptical about the technology's potential efficacy.

"It's just too easy to corrupt the data by holding your breath, moving around a little or even thinking about some random stuff, which wouldn't seem to make it very useful on somebody who's trying to conceal something," says Ed Vul, an fMRI researcher in the Kanwisher lab at MIT.

Other neuroscience-based methods of lie detection are also in the works, though experts say it is too early to know how useful or effective any of them will turn out to be. Three in particular deserve serious attention.

Like fMRI, near-infrared laser spectroscopy provides a way to measure changes in blood flow in some parts of the brain without the complex apparatus of an MRI machine. The basis of the technology is the measurement of how near-infrared light is scattered or absorbed by various materials. Small devices are attached to the subject's skull that shine near-infrared light through the skull and into the brain. The pattern of scattering reveals the pattern of blood flow through the outer regions of the brain.

Researchers hope to use the technique to perform something like an fMRI scan without the cost and inconvenience of an MRI machine. Though widely discussed in the media, however, there have been no peer-reviewed publications on the technique, experts say, so its potential value is hard to evaluate.

FACING THE LIES

Another technique, championed by retired University of California at San Francisco psychology professor Paul Ekman, is based on an analysis of fleeting micro-expressions on a subject's face, which Ekman claims can detect deception with substantial accuracy.

Ekman, who achieved fame through his work establishing the universality of some primary human facial expressions, such as anger, disgust, fear and joy, helped the Transportation Security Administration set up a behavioral screening program using the technique at about a dozen U.S. airports. (Ekman's work is also the basis for the television show Lie to Me, which stars Tim Roth as a criminal specialist who studies facial expressions and involuntary body language to determine when someone is lying.)

Ekman has been working on the use of facial micro-expressions to detect deception since the 1960s, but he has not published much of his research in peer-reviewed publications. He has not done so, he says, in order to keep it from falling into the wrong hands. As a consequence, his research has not been subject to independent analysis, making its value difficult to assess, experts say.

If it works, however, the technique would have the advantage of not requiring any obvious intervention with a suspect. And it could plausibly be used surreptitiously, through undetected videotaping of the suspect's face during questioning.

Another potentially fruitful avenue of deception-related research is known as periorbital thermography. Its inventors, Ioannis Pavlidis, a computer scientist at the University of Houston, and Dr. James Levine, an endocrinologist at the Mayo Clinic, claim that rapid eye movements associated with the stress of lying increase blood flow to--and hence the temperature of--the area around the eyes.

As with Ekman's facial micro-expressions, this approach potentially could be used without a subject's knowledge or cooperation. But the jury is still out on its possible effectiveness.

Greely says nobody but the inventors seems to be working on the technology. And the National Research Council, in a 2002 report on the polygraph and other lie detection technologies, called the testing to date a "flawed and incomplete evaluation" that "does not provide acceptable scientific evidence" to support its use in detecting deception.

Many experts believe that the government is secretly funding research into deception-related technology for defense and national security purposes under the Pentagon's so-called black budget, a multibillion-dollar annual expenditure that covers clandestine programs related to intelligence gathering, covert operations and weapons development.

"There is no way of knowing how much of that is being spent on what," Greely says, "but it's safe to say that a lot of money is going into neuroscience-based deception research, which the defense services have long had an interest in."

Because of the magnitude of the issues involved, some experts have called for a moratorium on the admission of such evidence until the scientific community has reached some form of consensus on its accuracy and reliability--and the courts and the public have had a chance to consider whether they really want such evidence admitted.

Such a delay, Moriarty says, would provide time for additional peer review, the replication of results, robust disagreements and the discovery of any unanticipated consequences of allowing such evidence into court.

Others argue for a ban on all nonresearch use of neuroscience-based lie detection technology until a particular method has been fully vetted in the peer-reviewed scientific literature and proved to be safe and effective.

Greely proposes a pre-market approval process similar to that used by the Food and Drug Administration in its governing of the introduction of new drugs.

"We need to prevent the use of unreliable technologies and develop fully detailed information about the limits of accuracy of even reliable lie detection," he says. "Otherwise, honest people may be treated unfairly based on negative tests; dishonest people may go free."

For more watch a video symposium on new lie detection technology ABAJournal.com/magazine

Part 5

THE CRIME LAB
AND BALLISTICS

26

Inside the DoD's Crime Lab
Digging for Digital Dirt

Deborah Radcliff

Digital evidence comes in all shapes and sizes: pallets full of computers, a hard drive with an AK-47 bullet hole in it, audio tapes fished out of the ocean, mangled floppies, garbled 911 calls.

Whenever a U.S. government agency investigating a crime or a cybercrime has digital evidence that's too difficult to analyze, they send it to the Department of Defense computer forensics lab.

The evidence can arrive in a military vehicle, via FedEx or through the U.S. Postal Service. However it gets there, it's accepted at the loading dock of an unmarked commercial building on the outskirts of Baltimore.

It's then logged and sent to an evidence custodian, who inventories, tags and stores it in a locked cage.

Network World was invited into the Defense Computer Forensics Lab (DCFL) for an inside look at how computer investigators at the cutting edge are using digital evidence to help solve crimes.

Source: Inside the DoD's crime lab: Digging for digital dirt. Network World, March 8, 2004.

The purpose of the lab is to analyze evidence gathered at crime scenes involving the military. Whatever crimes occur in the civilian world, you also see in the military. It could be homicide, child pornography, identity theft, counterfeiting, misconduct, terrorism, espionage, contractor fraud or misuse of government property.

With these crimes, there's often digital evidence in cell phones, pagers, PDAs, geo-mapping systems, digital cameras, cockpit recording systems and anything else with flash memory or ROM.

"We estimate that 95% of criminals leave digital evidence at the scene," says Donald Flynn, attorney adviser for the Defense Department Cyber Crime Center, which houses the DCFL.

That evidence must be able to stand up in court, particularly now that judges and attorneys are becoming savvy enough to start asking questions about the integrity of digital evidence. The DCFL addresses this through rigorous training and advanced tools such as certified, high-capacity extraction and imaging processes and tools.

INSIDE THE LAB

My tour guide at the high-security lab pushed a button at the double-door entryway into the lab that triggered blue ceiling lights, which blinked incessantly to alert technicians that unclassified visitors were on the premises.

The lab includes your standard office cubicles, but every cube is outfitted with state-of-the-art processors, multi-system server stacks and 42-inch flat-screen monitors.

"Some of the evidence comes in on pallets - cases full of servers, CPUs, RAID disk arrays, floppy diskettes, Palm Pilots, digital cameras," says special agent Bob Renko, director of operations for the lab. "We've even gotten evidence in buckets of water - for example, video tapes recovered from jets crashing into the sea during training exercises."

The first stage in evidence extraction is digital imaging. This is trickier than it sounds because contents can be altered in the process - such as adding a date stamp when copying a hard drive, thus tainting the evidence and rendering it inadmissible.

Then there's the sheer volume of data. In 1999, analysts examined their first terabyte-sized case when they received a palette of computers belonging to a defense contractor accused of violating Environmental Protection Agency guidelines in its handling of toxic waste. If analysts had tried to use technology that copied and examined one drive at a time, they still would be investigating that case, says the lab's director, Lt. Col. Ken Zatyko, special agent with the Air Force Office of Special Investigation.

So analysts created their own script, which moves images of all the media into one place. In this location, searching and extraction is conducted across all the data simultaneously using the same search phrase.

Last month, the lab received several palettes, containing more than 3T bytes of data to image and extract. The evidence, which filled a 20-by-10-foot windowless room, required its own storage-area network.

The recovery process begins with entry-level technicians checking evidence out of lockup. Then they create bit-stream mirror images onto cleaned hard drives to prevent contamination.

They make the copies using a modified Linux tool dubbed DCFL Data Dump. The tool is akin to private-sector imaging tools such as SafeBack, which takes a mathematical hash of the image and compares it to the original hash to prove the image is an exact replica.

CRIMES AND MISDEMEANORS

The busiest unit in the lab is Major Crimes and Safety, which handles criminal cases involving digital media. The forensic analysts in this unit work in open cubicles, each with two Windows 2000 workstations, one to search the imaged data and another to store recovered evidence or for when they're working two cases at once.

Renko says the agency's extraction tools work in a forensically sound manner across computers and PDAs, but become problematic when it comes to cell phones and pagers.

"At least one time, we've had to work directly with the telephone manufacturer to successfully retrieve data," he says.

For computer examinations, the agency's standard data search and extraction suite of tools is called iLook, which is licensed by the Treasury Department. A private-sector equivalent would be EnCase.

Bill (for security reasons, analysts are only allowed to give their first names) is an advanced forensics examiner and former metropolitan detective in Washington, D.C. He explains how the tool conducts keyword searches, and reassembles damaged and erased files, e-mails, attachments, temporary Internet files, data files and renamed files into a list of searchable files.

"Say you have a contractor using sub-standard explosive bolts, which are critical to pilot safety because they're what makes the cockpit lid fly off in an emergency ejection. We know the cost of quality bolts should be about $100. We can do keyword searches through their accounting systems on 'explosive bolts,' to see what they're actually paying for them," Bill says. "Or, if we have a child porn case, we can order up a thumbnail view of all Internet cached files across multiple drives to see what's been downloaded."

As Bill finishes talking, a long list of files appears in the search window of his workstation. Six suspicious files are highlighted in yellow, indicating that the search phrases were found in those files.

HARDWARE MAGICIANS

Shortly after it became operational in 1998, the lab received a classified hard drive that seemed impossibly damaged. An outside firm estimated it would cost $250,000 to repair. Renko balked.

"We figured it was more feasible to train our own people to repair hard drives," Renko says, while pointing out lockers where evidence is stored when not being processing.

He stops in a small room with two Plexiglas-enclosed clean areas where technicians have soldered mutilated floppies and repaired hard drives that have been thrown off balconies and even shot with AK-47s, as in one recent battlefield case. The data where the bullet holes and solder marks are can't be recovered, but the rest can, Zatyko says.

The intrusion-analysis squad occupies the rear section of the lab, where examiners, who work primarily on Linux systems, investigate hacks on Defense Department networks.

"Our first job is to find out how the computer was intruded upon and what data was accessed by the intruder," says "Sig," who was recruited from his job as head of information security for a university. "For the information assurance part, we tell our client agencies what their entry point was and what needs to be patched to protect from future hacks."

Sig pulls up an advanced tool named Starlight. A multi-colored, three-dimensional map pops up: Each of its lines represent a separate connection made into the defense network and each color representing a different protocol.

"We've had entire underground hacker ISPs coming at us," Sig explains. Color-coding protocols makes it easier to determine which computer is sending which attack. "For example, the exploit in this case ran over HTTPS, so we color-coded all the HTTP proxy traffic in red. Then we can see that three of these IPs coming at us are involved in that type of traffic," he says.

In this case, the hackers were caught and prosecuted, and the entire hacking group disappeared from the Internet underground, he says.

As examiners trace hackers back to different hops and examine those boxes, they run into new variants of hacker tools stored on those computers that haven't been reported by tracking services such as CERT and Bugtraq.

The new hacker tools are added to the unit's malicious logic database, which will then detect them if they're used in future cases.

Furthermore, the database helps analysts spot similarities when multiple attacks are hitting different Defense Department networks at the same time, indicative of a large-scale attack by one source. Such cases are then reported to the Joint Task Force on Computer Network Operations.

154

In recent months, law enforcement agents from Australia, Canada, Germany, Hong Kong, Singapore, the U.K. and other nations have toured the facility to better develop their own cybercrime units. U.S. attorneys, judges and law enforcement agencies also frequently call for technical clarification. (For example, a recent call came in from a judge who needed to know the difference between evidence recovered from a cached memory vs. evidence found in a file on the hard drive.)

As more cases involve digital evidence, the need for sophisticated digital forensics capability throughout the legal system will continue to grow, says Gail Thackery, U.S. Attorney for the state of Arizona. Thackery has prosecuted a number of computer-related crime cases and teaches at ACIS International Association of Computer Investigative Specialists.

"Police used to worry about guns and blood and chemical evidence, but now every case in America has a computer involved in it. The legal system is hungry for experts at digital evidence," she says.

"So computer forensics training and careers are going to be hot for a long time," she adds.

27

The Current Status of GSR Examinations
Gunshot Residue Examinations

Michael Trimpe

Research and advancements in technology have brought changes to gunshot residue (GSR) examinations over the past several years. While the Final Report on Particle Analysis for Gunshot Residue Detection, released in 1977, still stands as an excellent comprehensive report on the analysis and interpretation of primer GSR, additional research and development have led to improvements and refinements in how authorities detect GSR. (1) Particle analysis by scanning electron microscopy/energy dispersive x-ray spectrometry (SEM/EDS) has become the preferred method of analysis over bulk techniques, such as atomic absorption, because SEM/EDS provides increased specificity, as well as the ability to conduct analysis without chemicals. Recently, technological advances have made particle analysis quicker and easier, but most current research involves the interpretation of results.

Communication among SEM gunshot residue analysts has inspired research and studies that, in turn, have brought about enhanced understanding and increased confidence in GSR interpretation.

Source: The Current Status of GSR examinations. FBI Law Enforcement Bulletin, May 2011, v80 i5 p24(9).

Conversely, media coverage of specific cases involving GSR, as well as articles in nonpeer-reviewed publications, have led to confusion about the meaning of GSR findings. (2) Reputable scientists always have reported that the finding of GSR cannot indicate the shooter, yet members of the media usually seem surprised to learn that. Nevertheless, GSR findings continue to add value simply because numerous population studies have shown that GSR is not normally found on the average person. (3) In addition, exhaustive study into the search for false positive results has strengthened the opinion that SEM/EDS particle analysis can attribute the source of certain particles to the discharge of a firearm.

PRIMER GSR

A discussion of the collection, analysis, interpretation, and reporting of GSR requires an understanding of the formation of primer residue particles. Most residue originating from the barrel of a gun is burned, unburned, or partially burned propellant (gunpowder) and contains metal particulates, such as lead, copper, brass, or nickel from jacketing material. Firearms examiners use this type of GSR to determine the distance between the muzzle of a gun and a target. When forensic trace evidence examiners receive a request to look for GSR on the hands or clothing of a suspected shooter, they search for residue from the primer.

The firing pin of a gun hits the back of the cartridge, activating the shock-sensitive primer, which ignites the gunpowder, forcing the bullet down the barrel of the gun and on its path. The heat and pressure within the cartridge vaporize the metals from the primer. Vapors escape from any area of the weapon not gas tight, like the breach area and muzzle. The heat of this explosive reaction and subsequent cooling results in the condensation and formation of tiny metal-containing particles. These particles fall on anything in the vicinity of the fired weapon, including the hands of the shooter, and typically measure 1 to 10 microns ($[10.\text{sup.-}6]$ m) in size (for comparison, a typical human hair is approximately 100 microns in diameter). Finding and viewing primer GSR particles require a high-powered microscope, such as an SEM.

Gunshot residue particles can be removed easily from the surfaces they land on. Regular activities, such as putting hands in pockets, rubbing hands together, or handling items, can wipe them away. (4) The washing of hands can remove most, if not all, particles. Rates of loss vary widely with the activity of the subject. Depending on conditions and activity, particles may be removed from a shooter's hands within 4 to 5 hours after a shooting event. (5) They also can transfer from a surface or person to another individual; the amount depends on the number of GSR particles on the contaminated surface (e.g., a person's clothing or hands) and likely will be a small percentage of the total number of particles present. Tests show that people standing within 3 feet to the side of a shooter may have GSR on their hands, whereas those standing 10 or more feet in the same direction typically will not. (6) This can vary with the type of gun and ammunition, number of shots fired, and the environment of the shooting. Gunshot primer residue also can travel downrange with each firing of a weapon. (7) Long guns, like rifles and shotguns, tend to leave less GSR on shooters than handguns. (8)

GSR SAMPLES

Investigators collect primer GSR with adhesive lifters, sometimes referred to in supply catalogs as dabs or stubs. Several companies sell them, usually as a kit with gloves, instructions, an information form, and tape to seal the kit when finished. The adhesive contains carbon, which colors it black and makes it able to conduct electrons in the SEM. Analysts also can use clear adhesive lifters; however, these require an extra step of carbon coating to prevent charging from the electron beam hitting the sample during analysis.

The adhesive is located on an aluminum stub fixed into the cap of a plastic container. Removing the cap exposes the tape, and the sample collection official can press the adhesive--without ever touching it--to the sampling surface. The submitting officer completes the information form, which provides collection-site data (e.g., condition of the subject's hands, known activity prior to collection, estimated time of shooting, and exact time of collection), as well as the type of gun and ammunition used in the event, if known.

Investigators should use one lifter per collection site. Some kits contain two (left hand and right hand), and others feature four (left back, left palm, right back, and right palm). One lifter can suffice when sampling an entire hand, front and back. (9) Lifters from separate hands can be considered and analyzed as one subject's sample at the lab. Finding particles on the left hand versus the right hand or back versus palm holds no significance because analysts do not know the activity of the hands between the time of the shooting and the time of collection and because both hands likely are in the vicinity of the fired weapon. Investigators can press lifters to the face, hair, or clothing if they suspect that the hands have been cleaned between shooting and collection or covered at the time of the event.

For sampling inanimate objects, like clothing, investigators employ the same type of adhesive lifters. The areas of the garment for sampling depend on whether the person wearing the clothes was believed to be firing a gun, carrying one in a specific location, or trying to conceal a gun in a particular manner. Analysts usually avoid excessively soiled or bloody areas of clothing as these materials can inhibit the ability to find GSR particles. Laboratory tests have shown that GSR on clothing will last considerably longer than on hands, but exactly how long remains unknown and greatly depends on the activity of the clothing and the type of fabric. (10) Similar to hands, however, washing will remove most, if not all, residue from the clothing. (11)

When submitting evidence, investigators must realize that forensic testing laboratories can have different case-acceptance criteria. For instance, some may not test victims, kits unsuitable for SEM analysis, or samples collected past a specified time limit. Each facility must assess the needs of the community it serves, the importance of the testing, and the cost of analysis. In addition, laboratories must consider the personnel, instrumentation, and time available for the work involved. As one example, the FBI Laboratory no longer accepts GSR cases because of a decision that its resources would serve its community, the United States, better when directed toward fighting terrorism. (12)

Case acceptance criteria applies to all forensic examinations, including those involving GSR, fingerprints, hairs, soils, DNA, and drugs. Therefore, it is common for one GSR testing laboratory to accept victim, back and palm, clothing, and face samples, as well as those collected beyond 5 hours, while another facility does not. Correspondingly, one laboratory might reject DNA samples for lesser crimes while another may accept them. A drug laboratory may not accept syringe or currency samples and might test only enough samples to reach maximum charge in its jurisdiction. A firearms testing facility may not analyze clothing for distance determinations, perform function tests on firearms, or compare unfired ammunition. Investigators best can maximize the use of GSR analysis results by knowing the laboratory's case acceptance policy and the reasoning behind it. (13)

CONTAMINATION

Police officers are trained to collect samples as soon as possible after apprehending, a suspect--preferably, before transportation to the police station--and to clean their hands and wear gloves when sampling suspects to prevent contamination. While law enforcement personnel could be a potential source of GSR because they carry guns, studies have shown that few of them have particles on their hands because they clean their hands much more often than they touch their weapons. (14) Nevertheless, police officers should avoid contact with a subject's hands before sampling. If armed officers collect the samples, a disposable lab coat, along with proper hand washing and glove use, can minimize the risk of contamination. As police vehicles and interrogation rooms are potential sources of contamination, investigators should collect GSR samples before transporting subjects in a police car or questioning them at the station. Studies have indicated a low potential for secondary transfer in these areas and that testing them occasionally may help prove the low risk of contamination. (15)

During examination, safeguards can ensure that GSR samples remain uncontaminated in the laboratory. Samples for GSR testing never should be exposed to the firearms area of the facility. Sample stubs are exposed only to the air immediately before and after placement in the SEM vacuum chamber. A positive control (e.g., a stub containing GSR) and a blank (e.g., an unused stub from the submitted sample collection kit or one free of GSR) in each analysis ensure that contamination has not occurred and that the instrument functions properly. To monitor the examination area, personnel place a blank adhesive lifter in the laboratory where clothing is tested for GSR. The examination area and the SEM instrument area should be located far from the firearms section of a laboratory. Additionally, no armed personnel or persons who made contact with the firearms section on the day of analysis should have access to those areas.

ANALYSIS

Analysis of the adhesive stub is performed with an SEM/EDS. At least 140 SEMs used for GSR analysis exist in crime laboratories throughout the world. (16) Usually, such facilities use a sophisticated software program to automatically search adhesive stubs for GRS particles. As the instrument detects particles of suspected GSR, a computer stores the coordinates of each one for manual confirmation by trained laboratory personnel upon completion of the automated analysis. Analyst-controlled setup and manual confirmation of results is tedious and time-consuming; the actual automated search of one blank stub can take 2 to 6 hours, depending on the instrument and chosen parameters. If a sample contains a large number of detected particles, the duration of analysis could increase greatly. Once the instrument finds suspected GSR particles, the analyst relocates and manually confirms a sufficient number of them. The examiner documents and reports confirmed GSR particles.

A particle must meet certain criteria to become characterized as GSR. Three specifications, in particular, determine if a particle originates from the primer of a discharged firearm. (17) The elemental composition of the particle is the most diagnostic criterion. Most primers used in North America consist of lead styphnate (Pb) as an initiating explosive, barium nitrate (Ba) as an oxidizer, and antimony sulfide (Sb) as a fuel; therefore, a combination of these elements in a single particle proves very significant. ASTM 1588 Standard Guide for Gunshot Residue Analysis by Scanning Electron Microscopy/Energy Dispersive X-ray Spectrometry (SEM/EDS) contains a complete list of elemental compositions allowed in primer GSR determinations. Second, the morphology of the tiny condensed primer residue particles typically is spheroid or shows shape characteristics of having been molten. (18)

Finally, how the particle relates to the population of particles in the sample is important in determining its source. Studies have shown that certain detonated fireworks, used brake pads, and exploded air bags can have particles with GSR-like elemental composition or morphology. " But, each of those materials contains additional elements inconsistent with GSR identification. Therefore, a comprehensive analysis of the sample can eliminate false positives, leaving GSR as the only possible source. In this area, recent research and studies in the search for false positives have only brought about increased confidence in characterizing particles as GSR.

REPORTING

A forensic laboratory will issue a report of the findings and, possibly, an opinion in certain cases. No universal reporting format exists because each jurisdiction abides by the rules and practices governing its court system. A section pertaining to findings, results, or conclusions contains the substance of a forensic report. These results must be not only scientifically accurate but written in terms understandable to a layperson.

In a GSR case, the submitting agency, attorneys, judge, and jury all want to know if the suspect fired a gun. Unfortunately, the presence or absence of GSR on a person's hands cannot answer that question. Rather, as the accepted practice, all positive gunshot residue reports include a qualifier, such as "The presence of primer residue on a person's hand is consistent with that person having discharged a firearm, having been in the vicinity of a firearm when it was discharged, or having handled an item with primer residue on it." Conversely, negative GSR reports often contain a qualifying statement, such as "The absence of gunshot residue on a person's hands does not eliminate that individual from having discharged a firearm." And, when GSR is found on an inanimate object, like clothing, a qualifier could be, "The presence of primer residue on an item is consistent with that item sometime having been in the vicinity of a firearm when it was discharged or having come in contact with primer residue on another item." A forensic GSR report also may list the instrumentation used (e.g., SEM/EDS) and the criteria employed to define the gunshot residue (e.g., elemental composition and morphology).

A laboratory report may reference three- or two-component particles. Most primers produce particles containing lead, barium, and antimony, including any combination of those three components. While two-component particles commonly form upon discharge of a gun, they also are more likely than three-component particles to be found in sources other than primer residue, like fireworks and brake pads. (20) When examiners find relevant particles, they should not include the word unique in the GSR report. Even though analysts may eliminate all other sources in a particular case, three-component particles containing Pb, Ba, and Sb have been proven not to be unique to gunshot residue. (21) Also, some types of ammunition contain primers without one or more of those elements. During a routine analysis, examiners also search for the components of these more rare ammunition types. Therefore, a laboratory report occasionally may list other elements found, and analysts perform a comparison of the fired-cartridge casing in that particular case.

When forensic laboratory personnel find GSR in response to a request, they must report it. While experts expect to find numerous particles on the hands of a shooter immediately after the subject fired a weapon, discovering just one particle with the correct elemental composition and morphology nevertheless constitutes GSR and should be reported. Few forensic laboratories use a scientifically established threshold for reporting gunshot residue results. In those cases, if the number of GSR particles does not meet the established level, examiners should report those particles. Further, the threshold (e.g., three GSR particles) must be specified. Having a threshold of significance may be helpful in isolated cases. For instance, the U.S. Army must consider that all of its cases involve personnel who carry guns.

TESTIMONY

GSR testimony can be challenging because of the difficulty in interpreting the results. An expert assumes the role of teacher when describing gunshot residue and its analysis. After instructing the court on the definition, production, collection, preservation, and analysis of GSR, the examiner then must present the results in a simple, truthful, and unbiased manner. The difficulty lies in the fact that while analysts can report that the particles came from a fired weapon, they cannot describe how they were deposited on the item. Examiners called to testify on GSR results cannot identify the person who discharged a firearm in the commission of a criminal act. A positive GSR finding is most probative in cases where a suspect denies proximity to a discharged firearm because GSR is not common to the average person's daily environment. A negative finding does not imply that the subject was not in the vicinity of a recently discharged firearm; it only indicates that no evidence of primer residue was found on the items tested.

Often, defense attorneys will raise questions at trial as to why GSR was not collected, under the guise that negative results would have been vital to the defense's strategy and ultimately exonerated the suspect. Investigators and prosecutors should not let this potential argument serve as a driving force in requesting GSR examinations that might raise more questions than can be answered effectively.

So, the question arises, "Why analyze for GSR?" First, the technology behind the analysis of gunshot residue is unquestionably scientifically sound. SEM/EDS analysis has existed for a long time and been used in GSR analysis since the 1970s. Second, studies have shown that average people do not have gunshot residue on their hands, but someone who fires a gun most likely will for a period of time. Despite efforts by forensic scientists to disprove the uniqueness of GSR to firearms, research only has strengthened the position of naming spheroid Pb, Ba, and Sb particles as having come from a fired weapon. While studies of contamination issues continue, the likelihood of transfer from another source remains small in most cases. The reason for analyzing for GSR lies in the fact that most trace evidence is not conclusive but supportive and circumstantial. Glass, hair, fiber, paint, soil, and, sometimes, shoeprint analyses cannot conclusively identify a common source between a known and an unknown sample. The fact, however, that authorities located evidence with a possible common source is worth noting for the court. Correspondingly, GSR found on the hands of a suspected shooter is significant and worthy of consideration by the jury. For a court to understand the significance of the findings, experts must discuss all aspects of the sample collection, analysis, and interpretation at trial. Sources of contamination and an explanation as to whether the analyst could account for any anomalies in the findings also should be included in the testimony. In some cases, the sample collection officer should give testimony first to provide context for the results that an analyst may report.

CONCLUSION

Gunshot residue examinations continue to improve through research, advancements, and more integrated communication among analysts. Further, technology has made GSR analysis quicker and easier. And, understanding of and confidence in GSR interpretation have increased. In light of the importance of GSR analysis to many investigations, these improvements are encouraging to the law enforcement community and the justice system.

To facilitate the best use of resources, field investigators should have a clear understanding of the utility and shortcomings of an examination, such as GSR. Communication with the laboratory analyst prior to collection may serve as the best gauge as to whether the analysis of GSR will clarify or muddy an investigative path.

Endnotes Omitted

28

New Orleans Cops Challenge Ballistics

New Orleans police sergeant's lawyer challenged an FBI investigator's ballistics analysis of the Danziger Bridge shooting scene Tuesday.

Eric Hessler, attorney for Sgt. Robert Gisevius, questioned the FBI's evidence collection and suggested it discounted clues that someone might have fired on police Sept. 4, 2005, during the chaos following Hurricane Katrina, The (New Orleans) Times-Picayune reported.

FBI agent William Bezak previously told the jury the bureau shut down the bridge for a day in 2009 and found bullet holes along the concrete walkway barrier and a metal railing. He said the rail markings indicate the shots came from the south or southeast -- from behind the civilians and near the officers' position.

Hessler keyed on one impact point as evidence a gunman was firing from beneath and beside the bridge, on the opposite side of the wounded civilians.

But Bezak replied: "I have no reason to believe that bullets were fired from that grassy area."

Source: New Orleans cops challenge ballistics. UPI NewsTrack, July 19, 2011.

Hessler also attacked the credibility of prosecution witnesses, including former police conspirators who have pleaded guilty and testified against Gisevius and his four co-defendants.

The prosecution is near the end of presenting its case.

29

Teen Faces Murder Charges in Chester after Ballistics Tests

Mari A. Schaefer

A Delaware County teen was charged with murder Friday in a shooting spree at a crowded Chester birthday bash April 8 that left two young people dead and eight others wounded. Kanei Daniel Avery, 16, was allegedly found holding a silver Tanfoglio Giuseppe .32 caliber handgun at the bottom of the steps of the Minaret Temple, Fourth and Ward Streets, where the shooting occurred. Ballistics tests tied the gun to the fatal shootings of Robel Laboy, 18, and David Johnson, 19, police said. Initially arrested on assault and firearms charges, Avery is now charged as an adult with two counts each of first- and third-degree murder, aggravated assault, firearms violations, and other related crimes. He is being held on $2.5 million bail. Calls to the teen's mother, Janae Avery, were not immediately returned. District Attorney G. Michael Green announced the murder charges at Calvary Baptist Church in Chester, where the Rev. Dr. Martin Luther King Jr. preached when he was a student at the former Crozer Seminary, Green said. "We are looking for nonviolent solutions to the problems occuring among the young people in Chester," Green said. Authorities are still uncertain of the motive for the killings, Green said. One possibility, he said, was a beef between

Source: Teen faces murder charges in Chester after ballistics tests. Philadelphia Inquirer, April 16, 2011.

166

two neighborhoods. Another was a personal conflict between Avery and one or both of the victims.

Detectives interviewed more than 100 witnesses in the case, Green said. Bullets recovered by the medical examiner from the two victims were linked by ballistics tests to the handgun taken from Avery, according to court documents. Avery initially told police he found the murder weapon on the floor, picked it up, and ran outside, according to police. He later changed his story and said a security guard who subdued him placed the weapon in his hand, police said. After the conflicting statements, Avery's mother, who was present, ended the interview, according to court papers. Police said they recovered photos from the teen's cell phone that showed what appears to be the gun in question. A second gun was found at the scene near the two victims. "We can't put that weapon in the hand of any individual at this point," Green said. Others who have been charged are Carlisha Johnnerah Coleman, 19; Gregory Lamont Santana, 23; and Derrick G. Hamlin, 18, all of Claymont, Del. They have been charged with assault, recklessly endangering another person, resisting arrest, and risking a catastrophe, according to court documents, and were being held on $300,000 bail at the Delaware County jail. Coleman and Santana allegedly hosted the party, which was to celebrate Coleman's birthday, police said. The party attracted as a many as 200 teens from as far away as Philadelphia and Salem, N.J. Many apparently were drawn by messages posted on Facebook. According to court documents, females were charged $5 and males $10 to attend.

A community meeting was held in City Hall on Wednesday night to address the violence in the community of 37,000 residents. Green said detectives received a "tremendous" number of tips, providing information about the case as a result of the meeting. The residents of Chester "have had it," Green said. They are tired of the violence and will do everything they can to bring it to an end, he said.

DATE DUE	RETURNED